This book belongs to

_____

I am wonderfully made, unique and special!

Love Me Don't Hurt Me

An Essential Teen Guide for Self Protection and Advocacy Against Abuse

By Jennifer Giscombe Williams

Edited By Angela B. Slack

Copyright © 2024, Jennifer Giscombe Williams

All Rights Reserved. No part of this book may be reproduced, stored on a retrieval system or transmitted in any form or by any means - electronic, mechanical, photocopy, recording or any other- except for brief quotations in printed reviews without the author's prior permission.

All scripture quotations, unless otherwise stated, are from the International Children's Bible online version found at https://www.biblegateway.com/versions/International-Childrens-Bible-ICB/

LOVE ME DON'T HURT ME
An Essential Teen Guide for Self Protection and Advocacy Against Abuse

Cover Design: Peter Leo Francis

First Printing: 2024

ISBN 978-1-7398830-5-8

Published in the UK by SelectArrowLtd.

www.selectarrow.net

Dedication

This book is dedicated to all the teenagers who will read it, especially those who feel unloved. This is your book. Enjoy it.

Foreword

This book, **Love Me Don't Hurt Me:** *An Essential Teen Guide For Self-Protection And Advocacy Against Abuse,* is a must-read for teenagers and anyone involved in their care and support. An essential aspect of this book is that the author, Jennifer Giscombe Williams, has skilfully addressed the 'God Factor' and used principles from the Bible to provide guidelines and signposts to help teenagers navigate real-life issues by providing answers to questions and challenges they now face or will experience on their journey into adulthood. Topics such as Sexuality and Addictive Behaviours, including the use of Social Media and Substance Abuse, are among some of the 'hot-button' subjects that the writer has carefully and sensitively addressed. One could easily refer to the book as a handbook for teenagers.

It is clear that the author, having served in areas such as the Women's Centre of Jamaica Foundation and Advocacy for the Rights of Children, among others, is very knowledgeable. She certainly grasps many challenges teens face and is well-equipped to offer suggestions and solutions. The readily available practical advice will certainly jump out at the readers, especially the teens, as they delve into its contents and interact with the workbook segments.

As someone who works closely with young people and people in the education and church communities, I fully endorse this book and unreservedly recommend that teens, parents, teachers, counsellors, or anyone who thirsts for knowledge acquire a copy.

Errol Rattray
President/CEO
Errol Rattray Evangelistic Association
Kingston, Jamaica

Endorsement

Love Me Don't Hurt Me: *An Essential Teen Guide For Self Protection and Advocacy Against Abuse,* is the answer to every teenager's cry for help, love and protection in a world where their vulnerability exposes them to abuse from persons whom they look to for safety and protection. This book will undoubtedly help them navigate life's challenges as they seek to find themselves and love themselves for who they are, using the biblical perspectives so aptly recorded, and find help when life becomes overwhelming through the in-depth information outlined in the book.

Each chapter, though not exhaustive in its topic, includes areas that relate to and affect the lives of all teenagers. It builds upon a spiritual foundation and culminates with encouragement and motivation; as such, it transcends nationality and culture as the topics are relevant to the society at large.

This book, though written specifically for teenagers, is multifaceted. Thus, it can and will serve as a resource and reference manual for parents and persons who work with and are interested in the welfare and development of the future generation.

I am recommending this book because of its diversity. ***Love Me Don't Hurt Me:*** *An Essential Teen Guide For Self-Protection And Advocacy Against Abuse,* not only provides information about love and abuse and issues that teenagers face globally, but it offers guidance to pilot teenagers in becoming the best version of themselves.

In addition, the author has taken a serious topic and creatively woven activities - games, videos, and poetry - into the book's segments to stimulate teenagers' minds while providing learning through fun to make it more appealing.

May this book be a tool to build lives to the glory of God.

June Alecia Cooper (Mrs)
Guidance Counsellor,
Kingston, Jamaica

Acknowledgements

Thank You Lord Jesus, for giving me the idea of the book and the wisdom to complete it. Also, thanks to my husband Gladstone Williams for his support in various ways, and all my friends and well-wishers for their encouragement and support.

I also thank the many people who have contributed to this book.

Trica-Ann Morris held a writer's workshop I attended years ago that challenged me to write books.

Faith Webster, whom I worked alongside in having discussions and workshops about Domestic Violence, Child Abuse and the Girl Child, also offered valuable advice. Faithlyn Stewart inspired me to make it more conversational. Douglas Webster provided suggestions in Chapter One and assisted with copy editing. June Cooper helped to concisely describe parents' roles and responsibilities. Thank you, Errol Rattray, for your foreword of this book. Also, thank you to June Cooper for your endorsement. My cousin Rosemarie Syndab inspired me to be the best I can be.

Finally, thanks to my publisher, SelectArrow Ltd. Angela B. Slack, the editor, who gave me an ultimatum to write the books the Lord Jesus Christ placed inside me. She guided the manuscript's development, spent hours editing, gave valuable advice concerning content, and contributed to some sections. Her curriculum development and instructional design expertise were invaluable in developing the interactive lesson structure and assessments. Also, Graphic artist Homer Slack and illustrator Peter Leo Francis brought my ideas to life with care and creativity.

Thank you all.

Contents

Chapter   **Page Number**

1. **You Are Not a Mistake** 1
   - i. God Created a Purpose-Built World For You 2
   - ii. God Created The First Family In His Image 5

2. **Do You Know Who You Are?** 13
   - i. Typical Challenges During Adolescence 14
   - ii. Are You Experiencing Sexual Confusion? 17
   - iii. Establishing Social and Sexual Boundaries 26

3. **You Deserve Love and Friendship** 33
   - i. What Is Love? 34
   - ii. What is Friendship? 39

4. **Do You Know Your Rights?** 49
   - i. Your Basic Needs/Rights 50
   - ii. Child Protection 58

5. **Are You Being Abused?** 65
   - i. Physical Abuse 66
   - ii. Emotional Abuse 72
   - iii. Bullying 76
   - iv. Body Shaming 81
   - v. Sexual Abuse 84
   - vi. Trafficking and Smuggling 98
   - vii. Spiritual Abuse 102
   - viii. Neglect, Abandonment and Rejection 104

6. **Do You Have Family Problems?** 109
   - i. Child Shifting 110
   - ii. Sibling Families 113

    iii. Latchkey and Barrel Children 114
    iv. The Changing Roles of Women and Men 117

7. Dealing With Your Problems in the Wrong Way 123
    i. Substance Abuse 124
    ii. Digital Media Use 128
    iii. Harmful Images, Information and Songs 132
    iv. Teenagers Who Self-harm 137

8. Are You a Vulnerable Teenager? 143
    i. Children with Disabilities 144
    ii. Children in State Care 150
    iii. Street And Working Children 152

9. Do You Feel Safe and Secure? 155
    i. Violence in the Home 156
    ii. Violence in Communities 160
    iii. Violence In Schools 165

10. Abuses Embedded in Cultural Traditions: 171
    i. Child Marriage 172
    ii. Female Genital Mutilation 175
    iii. Period Poverty 176
    iv. Child Stealing 177
    v. Teen Prostitution 180
    vi. Abortion 185
    vii. Sex Selection 189
    viii. Witchcraft, Cults and Occults 190

11. Are You Aware of Your Environment? 197
    i. Risk Assessment 198
    ii. Accidents in the Home 200
    iii. Accidents on The Road 205
    iv. Accidents at School 206

	v.	Natural Disasters	207
	vi.	Infectious Diseases, Epidemics and Pandemics	209
12.		**You Can Make a Difference!**	**213**
	i.	Roles and Responsibilities	214
13.		**Conclusion:**	**231**
	i.	Answers	238
	ii.	Endnotes	240

Preface

This book, ***Love Me Don't Hurt Me:*** *An Essential Teen Guide For Self Protection and Advocacy Against Abuse,* is written for teenagers 13 to 17, but others can also benefit from it. It is designed to teach them about abuse, guide them with godly principles based on the Christian Bible and steer them toward the love of Jesus Christ.

For this book, a child/minor is anyone under 18 years of age. A teenager is, therefore, legally considered to be a child. Teenager, I hope that this book will benefit you in many different ways, such as helping you to:

- understand what the Bible says about you.
- understand that you should be loved.
- understand your sexuality, who you are, and who God has made you to be.
- understand the different types of abuses and actions that hurt you.
- know when you are abused, what to do, and who to report it to.
- get a chance to add your thoughts and ideas to the book.
- do some activities to reinforce what you have learned.
- share the book with your parents and other family members.
- give you a chance to read and learn as well.

Teenager, you are not the only one who will find this book helpful, as parents, teachers, guardians, Guidance Counsellors, and other caregivers can use it to help them meet the learning and developmental needs of the age group that this book will reach and will further help to:

- address some of the hurt or abuses that you face.
- change negative thoughts, words or beliefs that can affect you.
- reassure you that it is not your fault when they are abused.
- let you know that help is available and confirm to them that there are people whom the Lord has assigned to help them as part of His love for them.
- affirm you about the love of Jesus Christ for them.

Teenager, you will love this book. It has the following:

- A reading segment to provide you with basic information about love and child abuse so that you can understand the real issues facing teenagers across the globe.
- A workbook segment to stimulate your mind, allow you to think broader, and help you explore the topics further as you write your thoughts and ideas. It will also cause you to reflect on some things that may have happened to you or other teenagers and help you to understand that abuse is not the will of the Lord for you.
- Activity segments where you can have fun while learning. Please use these sections to add more thoughts to this book so that it becomes your own.
- Scripture references show you what the Bible says about you and your situation.

INTRODUCTION

Dear teenager and parents, I am so pleased to have written this book for you.

I was motivated to write this book after the Lord spoke to me to record my thoughts and ideas concerning the abuse of children. I garnered this information after doing several workshops and public education sessions on domestic violence and child abuse in schools, churches and communities for about 15 years. I have also researched the subject of child abuse, so there is a lot of information that I am privy to. In this book, two teenagers are reading along with you while doing the exercises and applying the scriptures. They are called Abigail and David. Meet your avatars, who will guide you through your activities:-

Child abuse is a severe human rights and public health concern globally, as it is one of the most pervasive things happening to our children. Millions of children are abused daily. The print, electronic, and social media carry gruesome stories daily of children being hurt, killed or missing. This is not good for our children. Child abuse affects children in developed, developing and under-developed nations. It knows no boundaries and affects children of all ages, colours, classes, creeds, and religions.

Regardless of the family type, children can be abused in these relationships. The family type could be the nuclear family consisting of a mother, father and children. Then there is the extended family consisting of the nuclear family and other family members such as grandparents, aunts, uncles, and cousins living in the same dwelling or nearby.

There is also the single-parent family where children live with one parent. There is also the sibling family where there are no parents, but the children live by themselves, with the eldest having parental responsibilities most of the time. A blended family exists where one or both parents have children from previous relationships in the home; this could also be seen as a step-parent family. Grandparent families exist where one or both grandparents raise their grandchildren without parents. Added to the family types are same-sex families where two men or two women are raising children which they consider their own.

Irrespective of the family type, child abuse can and does take place in all of them. Children who are not a part of any of the existing family types may live in a government or private institution for children or on the streets, which can make them prone to abuse. Children are also abused at school, in communities or on the streets.

While conducting the public education sessions in schools and communities, I encountered children who live in some of the family types mentioned above. It was interesting to note that the teenagers contributed to these workshops by sharing some of their experiences. I learned so much from them. They filled the gaps with some of their lived experience. I was happy to have interacted with teenagers of various ages.

I carried the children's portfolio for about 15 years while working at Bureau of Women's Affairs, Jamaica. This allowed me to sit on several committees where I contributed to plans, projects, and programmes regarding children.

This book is a good learning tool because it takes into account my varied experiences with children. It will enable me to reach more teenagers locally, regionally, and internationally than I did previously. Your avatars David and Abigail are reading along with you. They comment at the end of each chapter and at the end of the book as they are champions for change against child abuse.

The chapters are arranged so that each builds on the previous one, strengthening the need for your protection and the need for you to be loved and not hurt by others.

Additionally, this book is a valuable family reference guide. I encourage parents and adults to read along with you to help you understand the information and explore the issues in this book further.

Disclaimer
Teenagers, this book is written from a Christ-centred and Biblical perspective so that you will know that the Lord Jesus Christ loves you, does not want any harm to come to you, and wants others to love you, too.

It is designed for those who understand or want an understanding of the Lord Jesus Christ (who I refer to as God or the Lord), who made us and wants us to know Him and be safe. All scriptures are taken from the International Children's Bible (ICB) online version to make the lessons simple to read and understand.
I hope you will enjoy these lessons and benefit fully from this course of study.

Best Regards,
Aunty Jennifer

1

You Are Not a Mistake

LESSONS

1. God Created a Purpose-Built World

2. God Created the First Family in His Image.

Chapter 1 | You Were Not a Mistake **2**

God Created a Purpose-Built World For You

We were created to care for the Earth and each other

Dear Teenager, what better place to start this book than at the beginning of creation? Do you appreciate God's creation? You should! It's beautiful! God made it for you to enjoy and take care of it. Genesis 1 and 2 outline the biblical view of creation. According to these scriptures,

3 Love Me Don't Hurt Me

God made the world in six days. The paradise God created at the beginning of creation is called Eden, which was perfect. Everything was built and worked according to God's design.

Thank God for His great job of giving you planet Earth, such a wonderful, beautiful, purpose-built home where you can grow up. God made the sun, moon, stars, sky, animals, and plants for our benefit and for us to enjoy. Everything on planet Earth is designed to sustain humanity's existence and well-being.

Our job as human beings is to look after the Earth, keep it going, and love and care for each other. This assignment to look after each other and the Earth is a tremendous task, so humans had to be smarter than all the other creations that God made if they were to do an excellent job of it. Firstly, Adam and Eve had to learn to look after each other well. We who are living now need to do the same.

God gave parents and caregivers the responsibility to look after you because He cares for you. When we don't care for the Earth, including its people, and cause things to interfere with God's plan for the

Earth, this hurts plant and animal life and human life.

The connection between God's creation, His love for you, and child abuse is that you need to know how wonderfully you were created and how much God loves you. As a result, you should learn to love and look after others very well, just as God intended at the beginning of creation. Learning how to love is what this book is all about—to prevent others from hurting you or you from hurting others.

Here is an activity for you:

Say how you can look after God's creation (the planet Earth and its people) so He will be pleased with you. Use Genesis 1 and 2 to help you.

_____
_____
_____
_____
_____

God Created The First Family In His Image

Humans are created to reproduce after their own kind.

Dear Teenager, let's take a closer look at **Genesis 1:2**

"So God created human beings in His image. In the image of God, He created them."

Considering the marvels of our planet home, God's most notable creations were human beings because we are made in His image and likeness. He made Adam and Eve the first human beings on the sixth day. Adam was a male, and Eve was a female. God planned to populate the Earth with Adam and Eve's offspring, so He created them with the ability to reproduce after their kind. They had many children, leading to you and I being born thousands of years later. Adam and Eve were the first family; God designed them to be the basic social unit of society.

Since Adam was the first male, all other boys born were males, and since Eve was female, all other girls born were also females. This was God's pattern in design. Each creation reproduced after its own kind. Life on Earth can only occur when a male **copulates** with a female, producing children. This multiplication of male and female has led to you and me being on this Earth where the Lord commands us to love and care for each other.

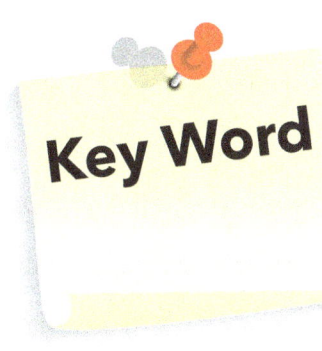

When it comes to males and females, it is good to follow what the Bible says and not be confused about your sex or try to change it. We should not change God's creation; if we do, we will create many problems that we cannot solve for ourselves and others, now and in the future.

Teenager, it is interesting to note that when God made His creation, from which you and other teenagers came, He said that it was good. In Genesis Chapter 1, verse 31, God looked at everything He had made and was happy with His creation. Wow! Just pause and think about how complex your body is and how effortlessly it works, then consider the planet Earth and all that exists. What a wonderful God you have!

Your existence is not by chance. It is not an accident. Do not take it for granted; you were carefully thought of by the Lord and created for a purpose. The Lord considers children His gifts and rewards, so He is concerned about how you are raised and nurtured.

Know that you are a wonderful part of God's creation and have a part to play in fulfilling the purpose of humankind. Here are some pointers from Rick Warren in an article posted on **pastors.com** entitled **Helping Teenagers Live Out God's Purposes**

1. Every teenager was formed for God's purpose
2. Every teenager was formed for God's family
3. Every teenager was created to be like Christ
4. Every teenager is shaped for service
5. Every teenager was made for a mission

Follow the link below to read **the online article for further details.**

https://pastors.com/helping-teenagers-live-gods-purposes/

Chapter 1 | You Were Not a Mistake **8**

True or False:

God created more than two sexes. _____

Every teenager was created for God's purpose. _____

Humans' assignment on the Earth is to name the animals, plants and trees. _____

God designed the nuclear family as the foundation of society. _____

What does the scripture say about you?

Psalm 127:3-5 says:

"3 Children are a gift from the Lord. Babies are a reward. 4 Sons who are born to a young man are like arrows in the hand of a warrior. 5 Happy is the man who has his bag full of arrows. They will not be defeated when they fight their enemies in court."

The Bible tells us that God created everything that exists, including the world we live in and all the humans who have ever lived up to now. You are one of those valuable human creations! God made this beautiful planet called Earth your home and wanted every human being to be happy and healthy, to love and not hurt themself or any other human in any way. These are God's laws for living. You can find them outlined in Exodus 20. They are called the 10 Commandments or the moral laws of God.

When you accept this as being true, you will surely understand how valuable you are. At the same time, you must accept that happiness is not guaranteed in this life because of human sinful behaviour. Sin occurs when we deliberately disobey God's laws. Disobedience carries the consequence of God's punishment. To avoid this, as much as possible, you should live according to God's law, enjoy a healthy and happy life and help others to do the same. You must also know for certain that God is displeased at you harming yourself or others or with others harming you because it goes against His plan and purpose for us. That being so - with God's help - you have to actively do your very best to protect yourself from those who may purposely seek to hurt you.

Can you imagine a world that does not obey God's laws? Describe what you think the world would be like.

_____
_____
_____
_____

Here is an activity for you:

Have you made anything that someone tried to spoil?_____

If yes, how did you feel?
_____
_____

Did you ever spoil something that someone created?

If yes, what was their reaction?
_____
_____

If you answered no to all of the above, create something you believe is perfect, spoil it, and express how you feel. The following scenario may help you carry out this exercise.

Create something you find interesting and then dismantle it purposely. You will learn firsthand how displeasing and hurtful it is for something you care for and took time and effort to design and develop to be damaged or destroyed.

Did you picture that you made something, like a drawing, your favourite dish or a sand castle on the beach? Imagine if someone came and spoiled what you made by adding something extra that you did not want. Since you manufactured these products, these people have interfered with the manufacturer's design. Did you find this to be a frustrating yet important lesson?

_____

_____

Hurting Ourselves Hurts God

In this Chapter, you learned that God created us in His image. We have feelings and intelligence like Him. If we cause harm to ourselves and others, it grieves God. God created this world for you to live in and enjoy. Regarding human beings, He made only two sexes, that is, male and female. One reason why God created males and females is for procreation so that the human race can continue by multiplying itself and filling the Earth with more people like themselves.

Living on the Earth as teenagers and having experienced some of the beauty of God's creation, is there anything you believe humans have done to spoil God's creation? Please note below:

_____

_____
_____
_____
_____

Something to reflect on:

Reflect on how we build our families and live in communities. Is there anything that we have done to spoil God's plan? What recommendations do you have for a better family life and community?

_____
_____
_____
_____
_____

Teenager, you are God's wonderful creation, and this book will take you on an empowering learning journey so that you can understand that some of the things that are done in society could hurt you.

These have marred the world and prevented it from being a better place for you to live in. After all, you have young, fresh minds and bodies, strength, resilience, and a will that you can chose to align with God. You can help make a difference by the choices you make daily. Are you ready? Let's go!

2

Do You Know Who You Are?

LESSONS

1. Typical challenges during adolescence

2. Challenges with Sexual Purity

3. Sexual Confusion

Typical Challenges During Adolescence

Key Word

Adolescence is the phase of life between childhood and adulthood, from ages 10 to 19.[1] Teenagers fall between 13 and 19 within this age cohort. As you move from childhood to adulthood, you will experience significant physical and emotional changes. At this stage, you will try to understand who you are and want a sense of belonging as you develop your personality and interests. Teenagers differ; some may want their privacy, some may want to cling to their parents and some may want to do things independently as they adjust to the changes from childhood to adulthood.

Puberty Can Cause Identity Crisis

Adolescence can be very precarious as it takes years; in the meantime, many changes occur within your body such as personality and emotional changes. Depending on how this transitional stage is managed by your parents and the responsible adults around you, it can be a smooth entry into adulthood or a psychologically traumatic and challenging time. This is mainly because of puberty, the process that prepares the body and manages the physiological changes that are necessary for human sexual reproduction. Puberty can cause you to feel very confused about yourself. You may lack self-confidence, feel that you don't fit in with your friends and feel isolated within your family because no one seems to understand what you are going through. This is normal, and you shouldn't be alarmed.

Everyone is unique, so some teenagers will develop faster as they move towards their later teenage years and adulthood. During this process, you may have many pleasant or challenging experiences. As your body becomes physically mature, you become sexually attractive, and this can be difficult to handle if you are not emotionally mature. These developmental changes often increase the risk of emotional and physical abuse from family members, friends or even strangers.

If you were born in the late 1990s and early 2000s, you are classified as Generation Z (Gen Z)[2]. Gen Z is a digitally driven generation where virtual reality is very present, and there is rising concern that opportunities for actual person-to-person interaction and the development of interpersonal skills need to be recovered.

According to the writers below, *'generally, members of Generation Z are tech-savvy, pragmatic, open-minded, individualistic but also socially responsible'* — An Hodgson.

'For Generation Z, swiping, tapping and scrolling are about as second nature as breathing.' — Dara Treseder.

Gen Z has grown up with access to the internet and digital devices such as computers,[3] laptops, tablets, and smartphones with various features from an early age. By the above definition, teenagers who fall into Gen Z are highly at risk, especially when it comes to access to and use of digital devices and social media, where they can be exposed to abuse.

However, even in the face of this challenge, they have the tools and the predisposition to be socially responsible. We will discuss these challenges in chapter seven, lesson two.

Are You Experiencing Sexual Confusion?

David and Abigail are teenagers who experience various issues as they grow and develop. Based on their experiences, they will make suggestions for you throughout the book. Now, let's

Chapter 2 | Do You Know Who You Are? **18**

look at Abigail. Like you, she is unique. God made her that way. What do you think makes Abigail a girl?

- Abigail has hormones that make her a girl.
- Her brain tells her body how to be a girl.
- She was born with a vagina as girls are.
- She has bigger breasts than David.
- When Abigail grows up and gets married, she can have children. Wow! This ability to conceive, carry and give birth to a child is amazing.

List other things that make Abigail a girl.

- _____
- _____
- _____

Take a look at David. He is a boy and is also unique. God made him that way.

- David has hormones that make him a boy.
- His brain tells his body how to be a boy
- He was born with a penis as boys are.
- As is the norm for boys he doesn't have large breasts.
- He may grow hair on his face as he ages, such as a beard or moustache.
- He may have a deep voice as he gets older.

- When he grows up and gets married, he can provide the sperm to his wife to make babies.

Write other things that make David a boy.

- _____
- _____
- _____

Human sexuality is binary by divine design.

As stated in chapter one, God made human sexuality binary; that is, there are only two sexes, male and female. No one has authority above God to change the binary sexes of male and female. God does not give anyone the right or permission to change His creation. Each sex should function the way God made them to function. He is God, and He knows what is best for you.

Children are assigned to their sex even before birth based on their anatomy and chromosomes and is often revealed through ultrasound images or other medical tests while the baby is still unborn.

Sex determination takes place at conception. Following that, when babies are born, the nurse holds up the baby, and if it is a girl, the Nurse says, "It's a girl!" or if it is a boy, the Nurse says, "It's a boy!" In lesson one, we discussed the visible signs to show that the baby is a boy or a girl.

As teenagers, you should not be encouraged or taught that you can change your sex. When this happens, it is a form of abuse which can cause confusion and harm to you now or later in your life. The Lord made the human body to develop physically, emotionally and spiritually. Sexual development starts at birth and continues through puberty and beyond. As you grow older, you become more aware of your sexuality, and this can affect the way you think and act. Your hormones play a part in your development.[4]

It is essential to know that some certified Psychiatrists/Psychotherapists have been diagnosing people as having **Gender Dysphoria**, which is a psychological condition where they are very uncomfortable being in their bodies in the sex that they are born with.[5] As a result, there is a community of persons who are advocating for the surgical changing of the sex of persons who are experiencing the psychosis of Gender

Dysphoria; this will interfere with God's plan for these lives.

There is a body of research that currently exists on Gender Dysphoria. Research has shown that some of these people eventually suffer from mental health issues, which can lead to depression, anxiety disorder and suicidal tendencies, among other things. Studies caution that this condition has caused much harm to many of those who have resorted to surgery to correct what they believed was wrong.

Here is a quote from one publication of the National Library of Medicine: National Center for Biotechnology Information published online in November 2019, *'adolescent gender dysphoria is increasingly common. There has been documentation of the association of gender dysphoria with numerous other psychiatric conditions as well as attempted and completed suicide. The literature is unsettled on specific risk factors for self-harm within this population.'*

Gender Dysphoria can cause many problems now and later in their lives. Teenagers going through this gender identity crisis need to get therapy and counselling.

The Lord does not want you to be confused or uncomfortable about your sexuality, and He does not want anyone to confuse you, either. You should know what the Bible says about you and adhere to it.

Establishing Physical Boundaries

Psalm 139:13-16 says:

*"13. You made my whole being. You formed me in my mother's body.
14. I praise You because You made me in a unique and wonderful way. What You have done is wonderful. I know this very well.
15. You saw my bones being formed as I took shape in my mother's body. When I was put together there,
16. You saw my body as it was formed. All the days planned for me were written in Your book before I was one day old."*

The Lord designed our physical anatomy in an exciting and unique way. Each part is interconnected with the other and supports the other parts. All parts are equally important. By examining our anatomy, we can see the body parts that make males different from females.

This knowledge is familiar to you, as you would have learned about the different body parts, their functions, and limits/boundaries in school. Please use this knowledge to help you function as you establish your physical and emotional boundaries in relationships.

Teenager, in establishing boundaries, you are sending the message that abuse is unacceptable. The Bible also gives you guidelines on how to function in terms of loving and honouring others and how others are to love and honour you. We will talk more about this in lesson 3.

Diagram of the Human Reproductive Organs

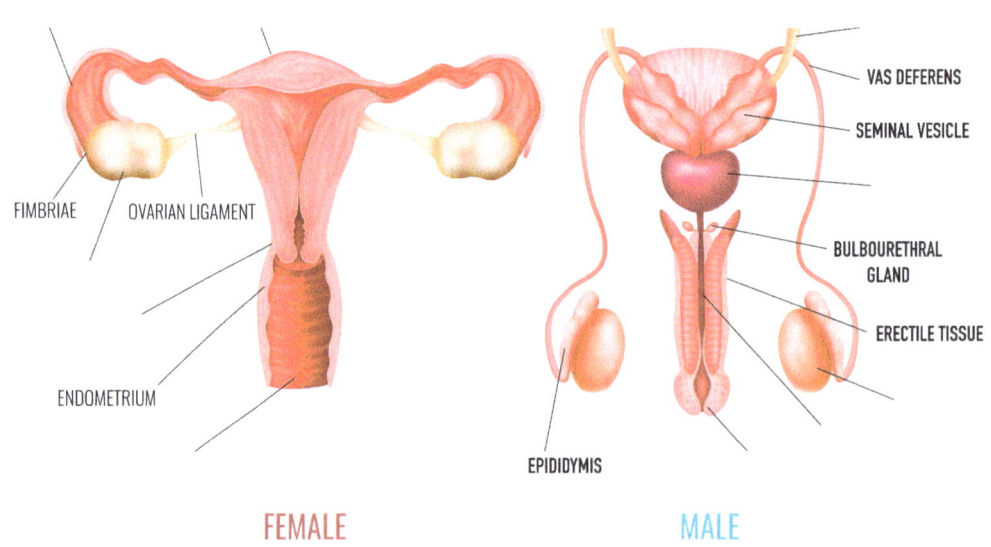

In this exercise, label the male and female anatomy to help you see the interconnectedness of the different body parts and their functions.

Our biological reproductive system is designed to ensure the continuation of the human species as God intended. It takes a male and a female to do that. God plans to have the natural development of babies in the female's womb, birthed by her. Every human fetus conceived is a miracle as it represents God's creative power at work in us. You are a miracle too! You should respect the **sanctity of human life**, knowing life comes from God and humans are the only species in all creation made in His image and likeness, having His very breath in us. From the beginning of the life cycle commencing in the womb to the end of life, the Lord wants us to care for, protect, and not hurt each other.

Part of the design of your reproductive system is to ensure the continuation of the human race. If you interfere with this design, it will malfunction and not fulfil its divine design objective.

Here is an object lesson

Most people drink tea from a cup, a very

familiar item in homes. A cup has a circumference, a base, a handle, and an opening for liquids. If manufacturers decided to make new cups with the handle at the base of the cup and the mouth closed up, then the users would not be able to drink tea from the cup, thus making it useless and dysfunctional. Just think of the human body as the cup. This would be very disastrous. Would it not be?

Please indicate what you believe would happen if you or someone interfered with God's design for your body.

_____
_____
_____
_____
_____
_____

How do you believe the Lord would feel? Please elaborate on your answer.

_____
_____
_____
_____
_____
_____

Chapter 2 | Do You Know Who You Are? **26**

"I don't believe the Lord would be pleased if someone interfered with His human body design. What do you think, Abigail?"

"I can only imagine how confusing it would feel. I will research how this affects children worldwide and their families."

Establishing Social and Sexual Boundaries

Key Term

How do you relate to the opposite sex?

Like other teenagers, David and Abigail love to engage in **recreational activities.** Physical and social fun activities are normal and healthy for them and you.

Spending time doing fun activities with your friends, with whom you have much in common, is very positive; you should enjoy your teenage years. Most teenagers entertain themselves with friends by playing games, participating in sports and using various gadgets. Socialising, making new friends, doing exciting things, learning new ideas, getting plenty of fresh air, exercising and resting are highly recommended for a healthy and balanced life.

Getting to know members of the opposite sex is also very natural. Still, you must learn to respect others and the boundaries that God has set to ensure that you honour and protect each other's dignity and not abuse each other. These principles are put in place by God in the Bible so that you will know how to act around the opposite sex and not be confused but aim to love and not hurt them.

Practising Honour and Dignity

Practising honour and dignity is a way of treating others to ensure their self-worth is never disregarded and they are never physically violated. Christians believe that this value system is essential in pleasing God, who places a very high priority on human dignity. Regarding how males and females relate to each other, one basic rule underpins all interaction and interpersonal relationships.

Practising Platonic love

In other words, boys, God intended that every female who is not your mother, aunt, or wife be viewed as your sister. This code of behaviour ensures that everyone is treated with the honour and respect they deserve according to God's plan for humanity. We will discuss this type of love further in chapter three.

The same rule applies to girls too.

Girls, God intended that every male who is not your father, uncle, or husband be viewed as your brother. **Platonic** love/behaviour ensures that everyone is treated with the honour and respect they deserve according to God's plan for humanity.

That being so, you would naturally look out for and care for your younger brother or sister, show regard for your older brother or sister, and listen to his or her guidance. It means that the boundaries of what is appropriate behaviour towards the opposite sex become very easy to determine and maintain as a society.

There certainly would not be the confusion and abuses society is battling today. If everyone adopted this code of behaviour, wouldn't the world be a wonderfully safe and pleasant place to live in? God's plans for us are always the best.

Teenagers, be glad because you are very precious to the Lord.

You are created by divine design. You are a masterpiece created by God for His glory. Everything about you was intended to fulfil God's purpose for you in this life. Teenagers are special, like David and Abigail. The Lord gave you mothers, fathers, grandmothers, grandfathers, aunts, uncles, cousins, other family members and caregivers to care for you. There are also teachers, guidance counsellors, coaches, church members and others. These people should love you and make you feel special. When they do not care for you, they are not doing what the Lord wants them to do. Do you agree with that? Write yes or no and say why you think so.

_____
_____
_____
_____

Chapter 2 | Do You Know Who You Are? **30**

Hi again, I am reading, noting the scriptures and doing the activities along with you. Remember you are special.

Hi, remember I am also here working along with you as you read the scriptures fully. Note that your body is made unique by God.

Your Body is Special

By now, you should be assured that you are a part of God's wonderful creation. You should be happy to know that the Lord made you unique. The writer of **Psalm 139:14** says, *"I praise you because you made me in a wonderful way; what you have done is wonderful. I know this very well."*

This scripture also applies to you and all the teenagers in the world.

Let's test our Learning

The Lord planned for you before He made you and made no mistake. Are you happy to know that your body is unique? The Lord made your body with various parts that carry out different functions. Some of the body parts for girls and boys are different. This design difference is how God made you so you can function as male or female.

Can you write below 3 parts of the body for boys that make them different from girls?

- _____
- _____
- _____

Can you write below 3 parts of the body for girls that make them different from boys?

- _____
- _____
- _____

You can try **Google** or other sources to find the answers. If you get them right, then you have done very well.

Jesus loves children, including teenagers, as the Bible says in **St. Mark 10: 13-16.**

"13 Some people brought their small children to Jesus so he could touch them. But his followers told the people to stop bringing their children to him.

14 When Jesus saw this, he was displeased. He said to them, "Let the little children come to me. Don't stop them. The kingdom of God belongs to people who are like these little children.

15 I tell you, You must accept the kingdom of God as a little child accepts things, or you will never enter it.

16 Then Jesus took the children in his arms. He put his hands on them and blessed them."

Jesus is still doing this today. He is still blessing children who are brought to Him. This scripture elaborates on how special you are to the Lord Jesus Christ.

Your body is precious, and no one should hurt you. Instead, everyone should love you as Jesus does. If everyone loves the way Jesus does, the world would be a better place for you to live in. What do you think about that statement?

Write your answer below.

_____
_____
_____
_____
_____
_____

3
You Deserve Love and Friendship

LESSONS

1. What is Love?
2. What is Friendship?

What Is Love?

God is love. Everything God does flows from His love. God loves us, so He gives. It is His nature/character. Love would not exist without God expressing or demonstrating it so we can experience it. Out of His love, God created humankind and gave us our wonderful planet home called Earth, to live and enjoy. He is our Creator and Heavenly Father who wants a close and trusting relationship with us as His children.

There are three types of love:

1. **Agape** is the Greek word for love,

which describes God's love for humanity as all-encompassing, sacrificial, and representative of Christian love. It is significantly distinct from brotherly love, erotic love, or emotional affection. Agape love involves faithfulness, commitment to morally correct behaviour, and the best treatment of the object of affection. It is described in detail in **1 Corinthians 13** below.

2. **Philia** is the Greek word for brotherly love or love between friends. It is also used to describe platonic friendships.

3. **Eros** is the Greek word for romantic or sexual love. Popular culture focuses only on the erotic and sensual pleasures experienced in this love and doesn't teach us to be responsible in how we share our sexual love with others. The Bible clearly states that sexual intimacy is designed to be shared only between a man and a woman who are married to each other. Marriage here on earth reflects the Holy Trinity and is a covenant between God and us to live and reflect his Glory. This is God's design to ensure we are happy and secure in our intimate relationship and build a solid family life.

Can you think of any issues that may arise in society when we depart from God's

Chapter 3 | You Deserve Love and Friendship 36

standard for sexual intimacy?

_____
_____
_____
_____
_____

Love is what motivates people to do good to each other. Where there is no love, abuse can take place. Love requires positive actions. According to the Oxford Dictionary, love is 'an intense feeling of deep affection or fondness for a person or thing. However, the definition of God's love is far superior as it is not short-lived or selfish, as human love tends to be. Agape love is described in detail in **1 Corinthians 13:4-8.**

"4 Love is patient and kind. Love is not jealous, it does not brag, and it is not proud.
5 Love is not rude, is not selfish, and does not become angry easily. Love does not remember wrongs done against it.
6 Love takes no pleasure in evil but rejoices over the truth.
7 Love patiently accepts all things. It always trusts, always hopes, and always continues strong.
8 Love never ends."

Can you imagine what this world would look like if everyone loved like this?

In **St. John 13:34**, Jesus says,

"I give you a new command: Love each other. You must love each other as I have loved you."

Jesus Loved us so much that He was willing to die for us to save us from the punishment we deserved as sinners. This scripture means that Jesus expects you to love others and for others to love you the way He does so that no one is hurt. The Bible verses above tell you that to love someone is to do good things to them and not to do, think or say anything wrong or harmful about them. Love is a vital human need; everyone must be loved by someone and give love to someone to develop into a wholesome human being. When someone intentionally hurts you, it means they don't love you. They are disobeying Jesus' commands. When you choose to love others, you are showing the love of God.

Let's test our learning.

Do you feel loved? Yes ____ No ____
Why did you say so?

_____
_____
_____
_____
_____
_____

Explain using **1 Corinthians 13:4-8** how you know when you are being treated lovingly.

_____
_____
_____
_____
_____
_____
_____

Can you make a list of ways that people have treated you in an unloving way?

_____
_____
_____
_____
_____
_____
_____

39 Love Me Don't Hurt Me

The table compares and contrast the difference between God's Agape love and human love. The first two have been done for you; keep going. Finish the table by giving examples.

Agape Love	Human Love
God loves us not because we deserve to be loved or because of our excellence.	We love based on selfish motives; we want to gain something from the experience or because we think the object of our love is worthy of our love.
It is God's nature to love, and He must be true to His nature.	It is our nature to be self-centred; we have to make an effort to think of others.

What is Friendship?

Key Words

David and Abigail are best friends, they have a **platonic** relationship. As they interact socially, they develop other friendships. They have a philia kind of love for each other. **Friendship** is critical in the lives of everyone, including you.

Chapter 3 | You Deserve Love and Friendship 40

Friendship develop when people love each other and decide to develop a close relationship with each other. Friendship is propelled by the love that friends have for each other. It can provide a source of support and shared moments of joy. They look out for each other and 'watch each other's backs.' Friends should try not to hurt each other by ensuring they don't say, think or do anything unkind to each other to spoil the friendship. ==Friendships can be used to manipulate others into giving us our way. This is abuse and can be very hurtful.==

Can you think of ways in which friends can hurt each other? Give some examples below.

_____
_____
_____
_____
_____

Here are some red flags to look out for in friendships and relationships[1]

- When your friends take you or the relationship for granted and expect you to be the one who is always giving
- When they complain about everything that you do

- When they monopolise you and your possessions/belongings
- When they only call you when they need help
- When they violate your physical and emotional boundaries

Maintaining Friendships

If friends do anything to hurt each other, they should apologise and make up quickly if they want the friendship to last a long time. Friends should enjoy each other's company without feeling afraid. Some friendships that began in childhood, like David and Abigail's, can last for the rest of their lives, even when they move away to places far from each other. They have to, however, cherish this friendship for it to work. Good friendships take an investment of time and other resources to make them last.

Here is a short list of 7 things you can do to build lasting relationships[2]

1. **Volunteer to support a cause that is important to you and your friend.** One cause that you could support is advocacy against abuse.
2. **Ask others for help.** This is necessary because you may find it helpful when you need help.

3. **Propose regular meetups.** Regular meetups keep you in constant touch with others. During these 'link-ups,' you can discuss your thoughts and feelings. Your friend can assist you in getting help if you are in an abusive situation.
4. **Develop communication skills.** Communicating effectively can help you express yourself better orally and in writing and will be helpful in times of abuse.
5. **Practice active listening.** It is essential to listen to your friends because you can help them sometimes, especially in abusive situations.
6. **Offer a helping hand.** By assisting those who are in need, you are more likely to get assistance for yourself when you need it.
7. **Practice forgiveness.** Forgiving yourself and others who have wronged you is necessary to heal deep hurts.

Determining Who is Your Friend

Interestingly, not everyone is your friend; some are relatives, neighbours, classmates, community members and church members. Although they may be closely associated with you, and you may interact regularly with them, their relationship is only considered friendship once you make it intentional. Some schoolmates share the same school space with you. Some may be your friends, but others may not be because they may not be close to you, and you have not chosen to establish such closeness with them.

Friends are people you let into your space as you set your boundaries. Setting **boundaries** can help to protect you from being hurt. Boundaries are agreed limits placed on behaviour, making relationships very clear.

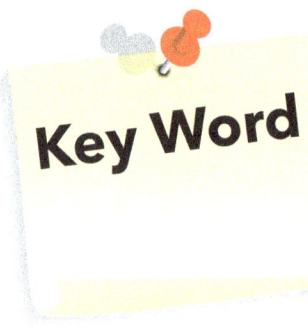

Let's test our learning.

Do you have anyone you can call your friend? Please write yes or no. _____

Please say why these people are your friends.

_____
_____
_____
_____

Friends are unique; sometimes, they like to spend time with each other and share similar interests and hobbies. Friendship is integral to physical, emotional, social, and spiritual development.

What would you do if a friend wanted to change your relationship with them to intimate love? Would you be able to remain friends? What are some of the issues to be considered? Write your thoughts below.

_____
_____
_____
_____
_____
_____

Friendship can lead to social interactions. Some social interactions that teenagers like can include games such as:

- Football
- Soccer
- Cricket
- Hockey
- Table-tennis
- Basketball
- Board games
- Electronic games
- Computer games
- Others

List other interests/hobbies that can create interactions.

- _____
- _____
- _____
- _____

The interests you share often indicate your personality, whether you are shy, outgoing, competitive or reserved. We all have different personalities; this should not cause us to hurt each other. Instead, we should love each other despite our different personalities, childhood experiences, or socialisation as teenagers. This is how the Lord made you to function and relate safely, healthily and lovingly to each other.

Even in sporting activities, you should care for each other as you are given a chance to engage, express yourself and develop your skills safely and healthily, where no harm is intended. Safety in friendship can be ensured or reinforced by your mother, father, other family members, coaches and other caregiving adults.

Please add words in the empty spaces below that can help to build friendships and make them last.

Love	Truth	Honesty
Care	Consideration	Trust

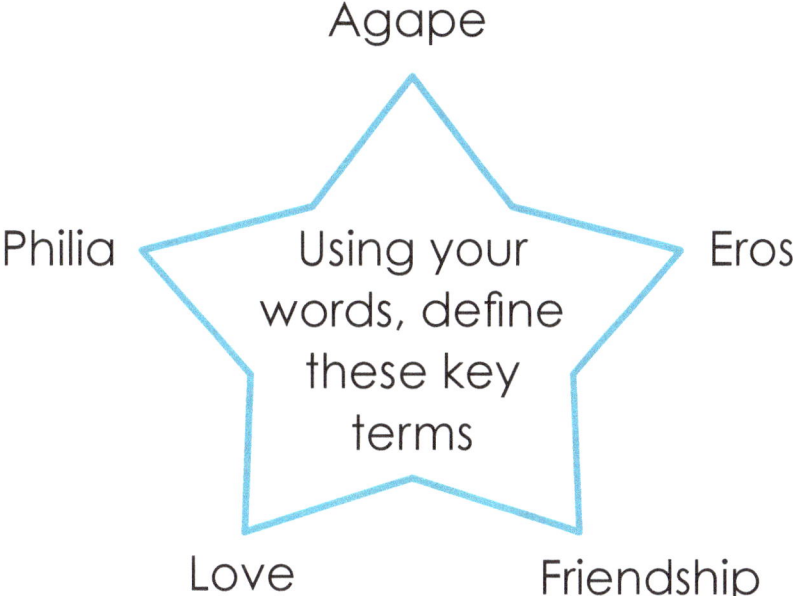

Love and friendship are pillars that can create a bond in any relationship. Like building any firm structure, they can help provide support and a wall of defence around you, especially in times of need. It is important to maintain good friends and healthy relationships; you may never know when you will need them. Let's be our brother's keeper because 'no man is an island', as the saying goes. We all need each other!

One of the takeaways in love and friendship is that no one should hurt you, and you certainly should not hurt anyone in all your interactions. Do you agree? Yes or no?_____

Why do you give that answer?

_____
_____
_____
_____

David, we're BFFS, right? #Lovemedonthurtme, dude.

Awwe, come on, Abigail. You know we're good. I've got your back.

NOTES

4

Do You Know Your Rights?

LESSONS

1. Your Basic Needs/Rights

2. Child Protection

Your Basic Needs/Rights

Key Term

Dear teenager, if everyone did what the Lord wanted them to do, you would not be concerned about your lives or feel alone, afraid or hurt because parents, guardians and other caregivers would be responsible and caring and meet your **basic needs.** Parents and other adult caregivers are responsible for loving, caring, and protecting you from all kinds of harm and danger. However,

Key Terms

sometimes, you may have cause for concern because of the violation of your **human rights.**

According to the United Nations Convention on the Rights of the Child, "**Rights** *are things every child should have or be able to do.*"¹ Almost every country has agreed to these rights. All rights are connected and equally important. All teenagers have the same rights. Sometimes, we must consider rights in terms of what is best for children, what is critical to life, and protection from harm. As you grow, you have more responsibility to make choices and exercise your rights.

With rights comes responsibility. We get more choices as we grow and mature. Based on maturity and age, parents have the capacity that children don't have. You remain under adult supervision and guidance until you mature.

Here is a real-life scenario that really hits home:

A family with a baby and a young child entered a restaurant. There was a high chair where the baby should have been seated, but the baby wanted to sit in a regular chair and refused to sit in the high chair. The parents yielded to the baby and placed the baby in a regular chair. Having been seated in the regular chair at table level, the baby pulled the tablecloth, and everything fell off the table. Hot food, everything went flying! Fortunately, no one was hurt; there was just a lot of cleaning up.

The object lesson is that the baby should not have decided where he sat at that stage. Based on their experience and maturity, the parents should have been the ones to decide.

Here is a list of children's basic needs or rights as human beings. Some of these rights have been summarised as outlined below.[2]

1. Survival Rights - the right to a happy life

2. Developmental Rights - the right to grow and develop healthily

3. Protection Rights - the right to feel safe and secure

4. Participation Rights - the right to have a say and express your feelings or point of view.

Child rights can be further broken down as follows:-

- Right to life
- Right to food
- Right to shelter
- Right to clothing
- Right to education
- Right to medical care
- Right to protection from harm and danger
- Right to a fair trial if in conflict with the law
- Right to play/creative expression
- Right to a name and nationality

Can you list any other rights below?

_____

Rights come with responsibility

All these rights are to be met by those responsible for you. They should supervise you well, listen, and respond to you correctly if you complain about abuse. Love, peace, joy, kindness and happiness should exist in your family, school and the wider community. If you are not allowed to experience any of the rights above, you are being abused.

What does the Bible say about children and parents?

Ephesians 6:1-4 says, *"Children, obey your parents the way the Lord wants. This* *is the right thing to do. 2 The command says, 'Honor your father and mother.' This is the first command that has a promise with it. 3 The promise is: 'Then everything will be well with you, and you will have a long life on the earth.' 4 Fathers, do not make your children angry, but raise them with the training and teaching of the Lord."*

As a teenager, although you have a voice, you do not have the right to disobey your parents unless what they want you to do is against the laws of God or the country or it is a form of abuse, for example:

- if you are being asked to lie or steal.

- if you are being asked to buy or sell drugs or arms or other dangerous weapons.

- if you are being asked to have a sexual relationship with an adult in exchange for money to help your family live financially.

Can you list other wrong things your parents may ask you to do?

_____
_____

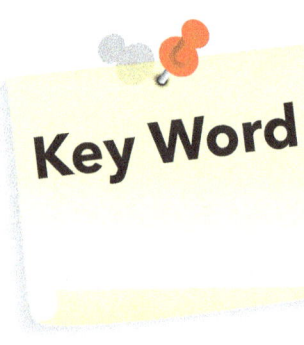

Living a Balanced Life

Do you know that we are **tripartite** [three part] beings consisting of:-
   a. Body - Physiological structure/Anatomy
   b. Soul - Our mind, will and emotions
   c. Spirit - God's life within us that is invisible and connects us to Him.

To be balanced and healthy, you must lead a wholesome life that considers each area of your being. The Lord did not intend any harm to come to these areas of your lives. We learned that social and emotional benefits derived from playing games can give practical value to our souls. Playtime can help relieve stress and emotional trauma, provide relaxation and enjoyment, and increase your chances of meeting new friends and acquaintances, which will widen your social network. A wide social circle may come in handy when you are in distress because you will have more people in your network to call upon when in danger.

In a safe environment, you can express yourself and feel emotionally secure through social activities and bonding. Your parents, guardians or caregivers should talk to you about the Lord Jesus and give you advice and directions for your spiritual growth and development. This Spiritual guidance is an excellent place to start in your developmental process. Please see Chapter 5 - Lesson 8, on Spiritual Abuse.

The Bible says in **Proverbs 22:6** *"train a child how to live the right way. Then, even when they are old, they will still live that way."*

The Bible guides parents in training their children because this is beneficial. Do you agree? What could happen if training is neglected?

_____
_____

==As a teenager, you should experience God's love, kindness, peace, protection and happiness by being a part of a community of faith.== When parents and other caregivers fail to allow you to develop an awareness and relationship with God, it is denying you your right to grow in a balanced way because you were born a spiritual being and need to connect with God. Many people who have not been given this opportunity to experience God in their lives end up depressed, distressed, and anxious as they are missing out on a whole area of growth that is necessary for healthy human development. God created us to worship Him, as stated in **Ephesians 2:10** which says:

"God has made us what we are. In Christ Jesus, God made us new people so that we would do good works. God had planned in advance those good works for us. He had planned for us to live our lives doing them."

Some parents are very busy with everyday life, so they cannot give you spiritual instruction and spend time with you in worship or spiritually fulfilling activities as they should. The lack of spiritual guidance can leave you feeling empty inside and susceptible to self-harm and abuse by others.

Can you say how Parents and Caregivers/Guardians can fail you spiritually?

_____
_____
_____
_____

> **WOW! I have many rights as a teenager.**

> **Remember that you have responsibilities, too. They go hand in hand.**

Child Protection

The Lord is mindful and concerned about children, including teenagers. His plan is that children be protected at all times, and He has stated this in several scriptures. He plans for children to have two loving parents to care for them. In the absence of parents, other caregivers should perform that role. Because of the constant and ongoing abuse of children, some protective measures have been put in place to address these abuses.

There has been a multi-agency approach in different countries in terms of addressing child protection. Governments, the private sector, non-governmental organisations (NGOs) and community-based organisations have all been fighting to protect children and keep them safe. Despite these efforts, several gaps in child protection exist in the different systems.

Key Term

When we talk about **child protection**, exactly what are we talking about? Did you know that UNICEF uses the term **child protection** to refer to the prevention and response to violence, exploitation and abuse of children in all contexts? Child Protection includes reaching children who are especially vulnerable to these threats, such as those living without family care, on the streets or in situations of conflict or natural disasters. We will discuss this further in Chapter 8.

UNICEF indicated that *'children experience insidious forms of violence, exploitation and abuse. This happens in every country and all places. Children should be most protected in their homes, schools and communities. Violence against children can be physical, emotional or sexual. In many cases, children suffer at the hands of the people they trust.'*[3]

Did you know that Child Protection is a concern of both local and international bodies?

> Did you know there are policies to protect you as a teenager?

> Yes, I know that the Government has a National Policy on Children to protect me.

- The need for child protection has led to countries having local policies and legislation, such as the *National Policy on Children* or the *Child Care and Protection Act*, to protect you.
- Some institutions are set up in different countries to look after your needs.
- The United Nations developed the Convention on the Rights of the Child at the international level so

Governments in various countries can use it as a guide to protect children.

- Also, **the United Nations Children's Fund (UNICEF)** was set up to help governments improve the health and education of children and their mothers.
- Some countries have Children's Services Agencies, Child Protection Boards, Child Protection and Family Services Agencies, Family Courts and other institutions to protect you.

Let's Test our Learning:

1. What does your country have in place to protect you?

   _____
   _____
   _____
   _____
   _____

2. Please research how the different agencies in your country manage child protection and fill in the blanks below.

   a. Name a Government Agency that protects children

   _____

b. Non-Governmental Organisation (NGO)_____

c. National Policy on Children
_____

d. Your School Policy on Child Protection
_____

e. Other Policies on Child Protection
_____

3. Based on what you have learned, why are official child protection agencies and a national policy important?

_____
_____
_____

4. Besides the different laws and Policies, the Bible also offers guidelines for protecting children. Let's see what the Bible says:

There are several scriptures in the Bible that speak to Child Protection.

Matthew 18:10 says:

"Be careful. Don't think these little children are worth nothing. I tell you that

they have angels in heaven who are always with my Father in heaven."

Mark 9:37 says:

"Whoever welcomes one of these little children in my name welcomes me, and whoever welcomes me does not welcome me but the one who sent me."

5. Can you find two more scriptures and write them down below?

_____
_____
_____
_____

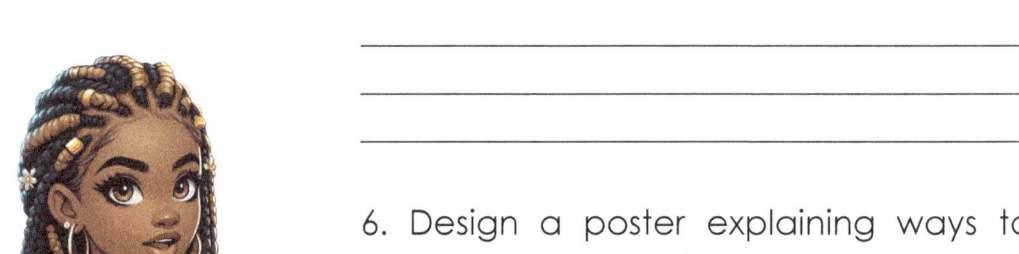

6. Design a poster explaining ways to protect children from violence and abuse. Include a Government Agency that protects children and their contact details.

NOTES

5

Are You Being Abused?

LESSONS

1. Physical Abuse
2. Emotional Abuse
3. Bullying
4. Body Shaming
5. Sexual Abuse
6. Trafficking and Smuggling
7. Spiritual Abuse
8. Neglect, Abandonment and Rejection

Physical Abuse

Key Term

Teenagers, I want you to understand that abuse in any form is about power and control. It has nothing to do with love; it is, in fact, the opposite. **Child abuse** is the deliberate intention of someone to cause you to suffer harm/hurt/injury to control you and cause you to be deprived of your human rights. In other words, it is terrible treatment towards a child by parents, caregivers or even strangers. It can be a single incident or several incidents that occur over time, which can last for the child's life cycle.

Child abuse happens when someone caring for a child hurts the child's feelings, emotions, or body. Strangers and family members or caregivers can also abuse teenagers. Most times, girls are more abused than boys when it comes to sexual offences. It is believed that boys are more physically abused than girls by parents and caregivers. Many cases of child abuse go undetected and underreported because it is done in private or by family members or someone whom the child or family trusted.

Key Word

These cases may be disguised as something else; the symptom rather than the cause is treated. Teenagers may also **mask** the abuse out of fear for their lives or safety or because of threats from the abuser or others who want to protect the abuser or protect themselves from shame.

An Example of Masking

If children are beaten and wounded and the Guidance Counsellor sees the wound. Instead of telling the truth, the teen may say they fell off their bike or down the stairs. The wound is treated, but the real issue is that the teen was badly beaten, so the abuse was not probed or dealt with.

It is not unusual to read, hear, watch or witness horror stories about children across the world as they hurt or suffer due to various forms of abuse. These incidents take place all around the world and range from physical abuse, including disciplinary beatings and other forms of beatings, to emotional abuse and sexual abuse, including rapes and other sexual assaults.

Children are also victims of spiritual abuse, neglect and abandonment. They are also victims of accidents at home, including household fires, accidents at school or on the road. They are caught in war-torn areas, used in wars, exposed to drug abuse and they are also exposed to environmental hazards and health threats. Additionally, we know that these result in injuries, deaths, and emotional trauma, among other things. These are all painful for children and cause much hurt and distress.

Each type of abuse can be a stand-alone, or it can trigger other types of abuse. For example, physical abuse may affect the body, but it can also affect you emotionally. The words abuse and violence are often used interchangeably.

According to the World Health Organisation Global Status Report on Preventing Violence against Children 2020.[1]

- Violence affects the lives of up to 1 billion children, with long-lasting and costly emotional, social and economic consequences.
- Globally, it is estimated that one out of two children aged 2–17 years experience some form of violence each year.
- A third of students aged 11–15 years worldwide have been bullied by their peers in the past month.
- 120 million girls are estimated to have suffered some form of forced sexual contact before the age of 20 years.
- Emotional violence affects one in three children
- Worldwide, one in four children lives with a mother who is the victim of intimate partner violence.

Teenager, since several types of abuse can be committed against you, let's start with physical abuse since it is more obvious than others.

Physical Abuse happens when someone intentionally applies force to your body. This can result in harm, injuries, or even death. Sometimes, this does not leave any visible marks or injuries on your body, but you are still hurt because the abuse goes undetected.

Physical Abuse occurs when others abuse your body, such as when they

- Hit you
- Burn you
- Choke you
- Throw acid or other dangerous chemicals on you
- Burn you with a hot implement
- Kick you
- Pull your hair
- Slap you
- Beat you badly

Write other things that people do that can hurt you physically.

- _____
- _____
- _____

Multiple choice QUIZ

Which of the following is NOT physical abuse?

   a. Hitting

    b. Slapping
    c. Pulling hair
    d. Name-calling.

What does the Bible say about how God feels when others hurt you?

God has promised in the Bible to protect His children and deal severely with those who harm them. Read the scriptures below.

Zechariah 2:7-9 The prophet Zechariah had a vision of how God intended to deliver His people from the slavery of Babylon and protect them.

"7 Hurry, people of Jerusalem! Escape from Babylon." 8 This is what the Lord of heaven's armies says: "Whoever hurts you hurts what is precious to me."

Psalm 17:8-9

The Psalmist had confidence in God's love and called out to God for His promised protection. Read the whole psalm to get the full context.

"8 Protect me as you would protect your own eye. Protect me as a bird hides her young under her wings. 9 Keep me from the wicked who attack me."

Emotional Abuse

Teenager, in addition to physical abuse, adults and children can also hurt you emotionally. **Emotional Abuse** is when people attack your self-worth or self-esteem or the way you value and perceive yourself. It can happen when they 'put you down,' when others say bad things about you, yell at you, criticise you, isolate you from friends or lock you away for hours, tease you, bully you, body shame you, or call you names such as...

- Dunce
- Ugly
- Fat
- Worthless
- Stupid
- Coolie
- Chiney
- Chink
- Black/Nigger
- Red Neck /Red Igbo
- Wierdo
- Retard
- Idiot

Write some names that adults or other teenagers call you that can hurt you emotionally.

- _____
- _____
- _____

Here is a quiz for you.

Which of the following is NOT emotional abuse? You can tick more than one.

a. Calling a child a dog
b. Putting down a child,
c. Pulling a child's hair,
d. Calling a child ugly.

What does the Bible say about God's love for you?

St. Mark 10:16 says: *"He took the children in His arms and blessed them."*

God loves to bless children to show that He loves them. He never agrees with hurting them.

Teenagers, here are some blessings adults can say to you instead of curses. The blessing below is taken from **Numbers 6:23-26.**

The Lord told Moses, "23 *Tell Aaron and his sons, 'This is how you should bless the Israelites. Say to them: 24 "May the Lord bless you and keep you. 25 May the Lord show you his kindness. May he have mercy on you. 26 May the Lord watch over you and give you peace."'*

Parents and caregivers can also bless you by saying the following:

- May you be emotionally healthy and happy in your life.
- May you have good friends who support you.
- May you do well in your studies.
- May you enjoy good health and fitness.
- May you grow up in wisdom.
- May you get much knowledge in your school life.
- May God protect you from evil and harm.
- May you fulfil your potential and achieve your dreams.
- May you have confidence and self-esteem.
- May you live long and prosper.
- May Gods grace and mercy follow you.

Have you ever received any of these blessings? Please state which ones.

_____
_____
_____
_____

If your parents have not blessed you in any of the mentioned ways, ask God to bless you as you desire. He is your heavenly Father and always listens to His children when they pray to Him. Tell God how things are for you and what changes you desire.

Dear Father God,

Thank you for loving me. Today, I am asking you to bless me in the following ways.

_____
_____
_____
_____
_____
_____
_____
_____
_____

Bullying

Teenagers, you should be aware that **Bullying** hurts you and other teenagers. Bullying has been around for a long time. A familiar ground for bullying to take place is at school or in educational institutions, even at the tertiary level. Many children have been bullied in schools. Bullying affects the one who is being bullied as well as bystanders.

Bullying can create emotional harm, but it can also result in physical or sexual harm. It happens when one teenager is hostile towards another and tries to control them by using physical contact such as force and violence and can also involve provocation and or intimidation of the one being bullied. It can involve name-calling, 'put-downs' or the use of harsh words, or instances where you are prevented from socialising with others or even participating in games or sporting activities.

Examples of bullying

When the victim's lunch or lunch money and sporting gear are taken away, or they are barred from entering their school locker room.

According to the CDC, Bullying is common in schools in the USA.

'About 1 in 5 high school students reported being bullied on school property. More than 1 in 6 high school students reported being bullied electronically in the last year.'[2]

Bullying can take place at home with other family members who want to control another who is considered 'weaker.' Bullying can also take place outside of the school environment, such as at the community level: in the streets near home, at youth clubs, parks, and shopping malls, especially when no adults are around. It can also involve extortion, where the victims are robbed of cash and kind.

Bullying can also be done through electronic means such as emails, texting or other forms of social media where harmful messages are sent to the one who is being bullied.[3]

Since the popularisation of the internet and social media, cyberbullying or technology bullying has occurred in this regard. **Cyberbullying** is defined by the

Oxford Language Dictionary as *'the use of electronic communication to bully a person, typically by sending messages of an intimidating or threatening nature.'* A teenager can be a victim, a perpetrator or both.

Typical Effects of Bullying

'Children may be reluctant to admit to being the victims of cyberbullying', CDC noted.

Some teenagers can become intimidated, fearful, withdrawn, or don't want to go to school or play with others as a result of bullying. It can cause you to become nervous and depressed, lower your self-esteem or cause you to isolate yourself. It may even cause you to wet your bed or pants at night. This type of violence against you can also cause you to perform poorly in school, cause you to become suicidal, or even cause you to hurt others or yourself because of the pent-up rage/pain you feel emotionally. Sometimes your parents have to relocate you to another school. All these actions can cause you to suffer.

Here are some red flags to identify bullying:

- Threats, name-calling, and racial slurs

by schoolmates, people in the community or at home.

- Aggressive behaviour or violence towards you by your schoolmates.
- Someone at school demanding your lunch, money or other possessions.
- When your classmates use personal/intimate/embarrassing information to blackmail you into doing their bidding.

All these actions by your classmates, community bullies or family members must be reported for them to be addressed. Sometimes, you do not tell your parents or teacher because you fear it will worsen the situation, as you will be bullied even further if the matter is brought to their attention. You should always expose bullying and never hide it. Hiding it may give the bullies a free pass at hurting you or others again.

Here are some recommended ways to deal with bullying

- Tell a trusted friend
- Speak to your parents, guardians or caregivers about it
- Discuss with your Guidance Counsellor
- If it happens at school, speak to the Dean of Discipline

- If possible, get evidence by recording, photographing, videoing, etc.
- Ignore the bully and walk away
- Walk tall and hold your head high
- Don't get physical
- Try to talk to the bully (to show the bully the error of his/her ways)
- Practice confidence
- Write about it, publicly expose the culprits
- Find your true friends
- Stand up for those who are being bullied
- Join your school bullying or violence prevention program

A girl threatened to fight me at school last week. I was afraid to report it, but I prayed to the Lord. He heard me and helped me to report it to the Guidance Counsellor. She was brought to the Guidance Counsellor's office for discipline.

Here is a quiz for you. Please tick the statement that best describes a bully:

a. Someone who calls you bad names at school so you become afraid of them
b. Someone who gets up and gives you a seat on the school bus
c. Someone who takes away your lunch at school
d. Someone who beats you up at school.

What does the Bible say you should do when you have been hurt?

Romans 12:17a says, "If someone does wrong to you, do not pay him back by doing wrong to him."

Also, Romans 12:19 says, "My friends, do not try to punish others when they wrong you. Wait for God to punish them with his anger. It is written: 'I am the One who punishes; I will pay people back,' says the Lord."

> When I was going home last week, some bad guys attacked me, and I cried out to the Lord, and they ran off. I reported the matter to the police, and they were apprehended.

Body Shaming

Key Term

Dear teenager, do you know that God made you wonderful? Sometimes, teenagers are emotionally hurt when they are body-shamed. **Body shaming** is when someone criticises your body size, shape, hair colour, eye colour or other aspects of your body. This can affect you emotionally, lower your self-esteem, and

cause you to lose self-confidence. It can cause you to believe that your body is not good enough. Body shaming can cause you to get depressed, not want to go to school, or maybe even cause you to stay away from others, or you may want to hurt or kill yourself or others. It can also cause you to have eating or sleeping disorders and other behavioural problems.

You are excellent and perfect in God's eyes and should not allow anyone to make you feel less of a person because of any aspect of your body.

What does the Bible say about how we should view our bodies?

Ps 139:14 says: *"I praise you because you made me in an amazing and wonderful way. What you have done is wonderful. I know this very well."*

This means you are unique, distinguished, set apart, different and made special by the Lord.

Let us test our learning

Choose the scenarios that best describe body shaming.

- Someone tells you that you look nice.

- Someone compliments your clothes.
- Someone says you are fat and ugly.
- Someone helps you carry your books.
- Someone criticises your nose for being flat.
- Someone refuses to ride a bike with you because you are too big.
- Someone says, "I wish I had your colour eyes."

Think of popular slangs teenagers use to body-shame each other in your culture. List four examples and provide positive alternatives below. Two have been done for you.

Popular Slangs	Polite Alternative
Abigail is a **Fatty Bum-Bum**	Abigail is a **Plus Size Girl**
David is a **Dwarf**	David is a **small boy**
1._____	_____
2._____	_____
3._____	_____
4._____	_____

Chapter 5 | Are You Being Abused? 84

Sexual Abuse

Key Words & Terms

Do you know that teens are not only physically or emotionally abused but sexually abused as well because of the high demand for sex? We live in a highly sexualised society where 'sex sells' and it is always in demand. This demand can cause predators to force themselves on you. **Predators** can be males or females, and victims can be boys or girls. They are mainly paedophiles, rapists, stalkers and groomers.

Sexual abuse is when someone tries to have sexual intercourse with you. Some ways sexual abuse can happen are described below:

- When someone exposes you to **pornography** and **sexting** (when someone sends sexually offensive messages through texting). For example, a nude picture, image or video showing a sexual act.
- **Fondling** your sexual organs is an abusive touch, and it hurts you psychologically, physically and spiritually. If adults attempt to play with your vagina or penis, breast or other

Key Words & Terms

body parts or touch you in any way that makes you uncomfortable, you should not allow it. If this happens, you should immediately tell an adult you trust.

- **Carnal abuse** is when adults have sexual contact with teenagers below the legal age of consent. **The age of consent** is the age at which the law in your country recognises that you can consent to sexual intercourse. The age of consent in Jamaica is 16 years old. What is the age of consent in your country?

  _____

- Sexual intercourse with a child under the age of consent is a sexual offence against children in Jamaica. The law may differ in other countries.

- As a child, you cannot consent to sexual intercourse because you are a minor, and your 'yes', according to the law, is a 'no.' When teenagers are raped or sexually assaulted, the laws of the land should protect you as you cannot know the full consequences of your decision.

- Rape is a sexual offence committed against a woman over the age of consent. In Jamaica and some other countries, it is when a man has sexual intercourse with a woman without her consent.

- Grievous sexual assault is another offence and involves penetration of the vagina or anus of the victim with a body part other than the penis of that person or any object manipulated by that other person. Please research what exists in your country.

- When teens are **buggered**, that is, adults have anal sex with them.

- When adult family members have sexual intercourse with children, this is called **incest**.

- **Date Rape** occurs when a teen is forced into a sexual relationship while on a so-called 'date.' Sometimes referred to as acquaintance rape, it is often overlooked and happens more often than we may imagine. Teenagers have friends or acquaintances they have known for a long time or someone they have recently met from the opposite sex. These persons could be a boyfriend, a fellow student, a co-worker, a church brother, or a neighbour.

"Date rape is most rampant among college and high school students, where the frequent overuse of alcohol and other drugs creates a large pool of people ripe for being taken advantage of sexually." [4]

How to Spot and Protect Yourself From Paedophiles

There are some evil people in this world. They will hurt you. Some of these evil people are called **Paedophiles** (ped-do-files). They could be male /female and be people you know or strangers. Paedophiles are people who are sexually attracted to children, and they aim to satisfy themselves while hurting the children sexually. Ask your parents or guardians to tell you more about them and help you identify them if you cannot.

Paedophiles do things like:

- Try to be nice and friendly to you, but they are evil.
- Give gifts to you or special rights and may ask you to keep them a secret.
- Show particular interest in you and want to play with and sexually touch your body parts.

- Kiss you or other teenagers in a sexual way.
- Ask you to leave home and have an intimate relationship with them.
- Have sexual intercourse with you or other teenagers.
- Take pictures of your vagina, breasts or penis.
- Threaten to kill you, your family members or your pets. If this happens, tell an adult in charge immediately.

If a paedophile approaches you, you can do some of the following to protect yourself:

- Run away to where there are many people around if possible.
- Fight with everything you have if you can.
- Scream out, attract attention and get to safety if you can.

You should tell your parents or guardians immediately. If you know the person, do not keep it a secret.

Who is a paedophile? Please tick the one that best describes a Paedophile:

a. Someone who sells candies to children
b. Someone who is sexually attracted to children
c. Someone who looks unfamiliar
d. A man with scruffy clothes and a long beard.

Sexual Grooming

Another subtle form of child abuse is sexual grooming. This can be a secretive activity where parents and caregivers may not be aware that this is taking place. According to the National Society for the Prevention of Cruelty to Children (NSPCC), *'Grooming is when someone builds a relationship, trust and emotional connection with a child or young person so they can manipulate, exploit and abuse them. Children and young people who are groomed can be sexually abused, exploited or trafficked. Anybody can be a groomer, no matter their age, gender or race.'*

Grooming can be short-term or long-term, in person or online. It can be done by a stranger or someone you know. Groomers could be family members, sports coaches, teachers, religious leaders, or otherwise. The relationship a groomer builds can take different forms. This could be:

- A romantic relationship
- As a mentor
- An authority figure
- A dominant and persistent adult figure

Here is some advice to protect yourself.

- Stay in control of yourself and your environment.
- Don't get talked into doing something or going someplace you don't want to
- Trust your feelings. If someone feels like a threat or makes you uncomfortable, stop the relationship immediately, regardless of who it is. Never allow yourself to be alone with them again.
- Never accept drinks/food you cannot account for from other people when on a date.
- Always let your parents or a responsible adult know your destination. Turning on the location app on your phone is very helpful in an emergency.
- Finally, always have your transportation or an emergency plan to get home. For example, money to get home safely if you need to leave quickly.

If you ever experience rape:

- Talk to someone you trust immediately; timing is crucial as it is a legal matter for the police to handle. They will need to collect as much biological evidence and physical evidence as possible to help make your case against the abuser strong.
"The evidence most often encountered in sexual assault cases includes not only biological evidence (e.g., semen) but also fingerprints, impression evidence (e.g., shoeprints), and trace evidence (e.g., hairs/fibres). Collect as much sample as possible from a single source."[5]
- Do not bathe, as this may destroy evidence. Report it to the police immediately. Get medical help. It is essential to know your status of HIV/AIDS and sexually transmitted infections (STI). You could also become pregnant as a result of the rape.
- For your emotional and mental health, confide in someone else if the person you report to first makes you feel guilty or disregards what you are saying. Speak with someone who can help you feel less alone. ==Most importantly, remind yourself that it is not your fault.==

Reports like the ones below are standard when it comes to violence against children. Read more online...

In Jamaica,
15-y-o Trelawny girl dies after being raped, beaten by intruders
https://jamaica-gleaner.com/article/news/20230807/15-y-o-trelawny-girl-dies-after-being-raped-beaten-intruders#google_vignethe

In Jamaica,
70 children have died violently in the last year
https://jamaica-gleaner.com/article/esponsored/20221122/70-children-have-died-violently-last-year

In Trinidad and Tobago,
Children's Authority: 4,000 cases of abuse every year (2020 article)
https://trinidadexpress.com/news/local/children-s-authority-4-000-cases-of-abuse-every-year/article_756805c0-2ac7-11eb-ba04-173577ae1886.html#google_vignette

In Sweden,
Daddy Detained: Unfolding Child Abuse Scandal in Älvsbyn, Sweden
https://morningsweden.se/news-owe7tgevjq0fgcpsm5uq/

In the UK,
Half a million children suffer abuse in the UK every year
https://www.nspcc.org.uk/about-us/news-opinion/2022/childhood-day/
Article April 21, 2022

In Kenya,
Action urged as national survey finds half of the Kenyan children suffer violence
https://www.unicef.org/kenya/press-releases/Action-urged-as-national-survey-finds-half-of-Kenyan-children-suffer-violence
Article July 16, 2020.

Sexual abuse of children can also result in teenagers getting **HIV** (Human Immunodeficiency Virus), which is an infection that attacks the body's immune system and weakens the defence mechanism, which can cause you to get sick more easily. HIV can lead to AIDS (Acquired immune deficiency syndrome), which is the late stage of HIV disease where the body can no longer protect itself against the virus. This disease can lead to prolonged illness and eventually death without early medical intervention.

Sexual abuse can also lead to teenage pregnancy, which can cause emotional trauma, physical stress on the body of the young mother and even further setbacks in your academic and developmental stages in life.

Pregnant adolescents (ages 10-19) are at higher risk of having emotional issues such as depression, stress and anxiety disorder. They can fall prey to drug abuse, have suicidal tendencies, and suffer psychologically from pressure to become parents too early. This not only affects the mother but also the unborn child. Teenage pregnancy can lead to the death of either mother or child or both.

Pregnant teenagers sometimes do not get enough support from family and the community because of the shame and taboo attached to it. This is an unfortunate reaction as two lives are at stake that need tender loving care.

Suggest ways to help a pregnant teenager. Read the report below for ideas.

Here is an extract from a UNICEF report:

"Globally, in 2021, an estimated 14 percent of adolescent girls and young women give birth before age 18, which covers the age range in this book. It further noted that early childbearing, or pregnancy and delivery during adolescence, can derail girls' otherwise healthy development into adulthood and have negative impacts on their education, livelihoods and health. Many girls who are pregnant are pressured or forced to drop out of school, which can impact their educational and

employment prospects and opportunities. Early pregnancy and childbearing can also have social consequences for girls, including reduced status in the home and community, stigmatisation, rejection and violence by family members, peers and partners, and early and forced marriage."[6]

Here is an assignment for you.

1. Name some other ways in which teenage pregnancies can affect girls.

_____
_____
_____
_____
_____
_____

2. Name some ways in which being a teenage father can affect boys.

_____
_____
_____
_____
_____
_____

3. Look for agencies in your country that offer help to teenage mothers. t's good

to know where they are located and what services they offer so that you can assist those who may need the service.

_____
_____
_____
_____

4. Name some other types of sexual abuse that teenagers may experience.

_____
_____
_____
_____
_____

5. Unscramble the words to see some forms of sexual abuse.

    i. fnoled
    ii. cinets
    iii. asutlas
    iv. nmoleostati
    v. ivolaonit

What Does The Bible Say About Those Who Harm/Abuse Children? Sex outside of marriage is a sin. God takes sexual abuse of children seriously as they are victimised by adults who, in God's view, should be their protectors.

In Luke 17:1-3

"1 Jesus said to His followers, "Things will surely happen that cause people to sin. But how terrible for the one who causes them to happen.
2 It would be better for him to be thrown into the sea with a large stone around his neck than to cause one of these weak people to sin.
3 So be careful!"

Every child is worth fighting for. Be aware and watch out for these perverted people, male or female.

What does the scripture say about the treatment of children in this regard?

St. Matthew 18:5-6 says,

"5 Whoever accepts a little child in my name accepts me.
6 If one of these little children [Teenagers] believes in me, and someone causes that child to sin, then it will be very bad for that person. It would be better for him to have a large stone tied around his neck and be drowned in the sea."

Trafficking and Smuggling

Unfortunately, not everybody who says they love you can be trusted. There is another set of wicked people called traffickers. Trafficking of Children is a form of modern-day slavery and a part of human trafficking.

The United Nations defines it as the *"recruitment, transportation, transfer, harbouring, and/or receipt, kidnapping of a child for slavery, forced labour, and exploitation."*

Key Term

Trafficking in Children is wrong as it hurts children. People who carry out these acts don't love you; they will hurt you!

Traffickers love money so much they will even sell children to get it. These children may be sexually exploited or forced into prostitution or child labour, be used as child soldiers in war or be killed and their body parts sold.

If you know anybody who is a trafficker, tell your parents or guardians immediately.

Here are some tips for you.

- You are to avoid strangers or people who make you uncomfortable.
- You should not take rides from strangers.
- You should not take gifts from strangers, especially food of any kind (sweets/candies or drinks).
- You should never let strangers into your house when your parents or guardians are away from home.
- You should not go on dangerous websites. Ask your parents or guardians if you have any doubts about any website you visit.
- You should let a responsible adult know if you believe you are in danger.
- When you go out, especially on a long-distance or overnight trip, always let someone responsible know where you are headed.
- Always keep the location app on your phone, set to 'on' to allow tracking of your location in an emergency.
- ==Do not begin a live chat with strangers who 'friend request' you on social media - BLOCK them immediately and tell a responsible adult.==

Sometimes, children are not trafficked but smuggled, although they can be smuggled and then trafficked at the same time when they reach their destination.

According to the International Organisation for Migration, 'Smuggling of Migrants is the 'procurement, to obtain, directly or indirectly, a financial or other material benefit, of the illegal entry of a person into a State Party [country] of which the person is not a national or a permanent resident.'[7]

Smuggling of children is illegal migration, which involves the movement of children across another country's border without proper permits or documentation. Smuggling involves paying smugglers to get the children to their desired destination. Sometimes, these children are smuggled alone while the parents either go ahead of them or join them later. This separation from parents can have short-term and long-term effects on the children. Sometimes, they are accompanied by parents on the smuggling journey.

When children are smuggled into a country, they are sometimes kept in undesirable conditions because they have no legal documents or status for the country to which they are transported. Sometimes, they are placed in shipping containers, in the holding area of ships or the cargo area of commercial trucks, or marched through long stretches of jungle.

They may be separated for a time from their parents and other family members, friends, communities, and the environment to which they are accustomed. They can be alienated, temporarily preventing them from continuing their education, and denied health and other social benefits because of their undocumented status.

The authorities may detain them and sometimes return them to their country of origin. This can result in much mental anguish. They can also suffer physical and sexual violence during the process. Some die at sea as well due to the capsizing of vessels that transport them or from suffocation in the containers that they are stored in or from diseases contracted during their jungle trek or from bites/stings/scratches from poisonous plants and insects or wild animals.

Let's test our learning

Which of the following is sexual abuse? You can tick more than one.

a. Rape
b. Incest
c. Carnal abuse
d. Hitting a child in the face.

Spiritual Abuse

Moving from physical, emotional and sexual abuse, let's look at **Spiritual Abuse**. Spiritual abuse is subtle. Angela Slack wrote an article in the SHARE Magazine issue from January to March 2017 where Spiritual abuse was defined as *"the mistreatment of a person who is in need of help, support or greater spiritual empowerment, with the result of weakening, undermining or decreasing that person's spiritual empowerment."*[8]

Some ways that parents can fail you spiritually are outlined below.

As teenagers, some of the ways that you can be spiritually abused are:

- You are not allowed to believe in Jesus or to practice your faith in Jesus

- Sometimes religious leaders abuse teenagers sexually, emotionally or physically and use the Scriptures to keep them in fear or to keep them silent and subjected to their abusive behaviour

- Sometimes adults misuse their authority over teenagers through coercion, manipulation, or force to get them to obey their demands by using the word of God as a weapon to instil fear and achieve their goals

- If you are not allowed to question any teaching or instruction given by a spiritual leader this is a **'red flag'** to spiritual abuse and could be a **cult**. You should always have the right to ask questions and receive suitable answers.

Parents and adults should pray for you and for your safety and protection as part of your spiritual growth and development. They should never try to force you to do things against the will of God or your conscience, which is what you know in your heart to be right or wrong.

Which scenario best describes spiritual abuse?

I am shocked; I did not know there was such a thing as spiritual abuse. Did you?

a. Slapping in the face
b. Beating the teenager
c. Stopping teenagers from going to church
d. Name-calling
e. Threatening the teenager with eternal death in Hell if they don't obey
f. Being forced to attend church meetings and activities at the expense of your studies and a good night's rest.

Let's test our learning

Can you say how parents/caregivers/guardians can fail you spiritually?

_____
_____
_____
_____
_____
_____

Neglect, Abandonment and Rejection

Some teenagers are **neglected, abandoned or rejected** by their parents or guardians. Neglect takes place when your basic needs are not met. This can affect you mentally and physically or hinder your developmental progress, which can sometimes hurt you for life.

Some teenagers were left by the wayside, roadside, in bushes, dumpsters, hospital nursery or other places as infants. Sometimes, when they are left at the hospital, and no one returns for them, they become wards of the state and grow up as teenagers in state-owned or privately run orphanages.

Some may be **fostered** or **adopted**, and some may not. This neglect and abandonment hurt these children increasingly as they grow into teenagers. The emotional pain gets worse if they are not given counselling.

Some were left to beg or to provide for themselves as young children. This hurts them, too. Sometimes, you are left for long hours by yourselves with no supervision. If you are left alone at home, in the park or at the mall, someone can abuse you or take you away.

Some teenagers are left alone for long hours or days when parents who are addicted to drugs disappear leaving their children on their own because they are too **'high'** on drugs, to go home, and their whereabouts are unknown. Also, single parents often leave children without adult supervision for long hours to seek overtime pay at work, work back-to-back shifts, or seek seasonal jobs that pay higher rates. It is not unusual for social workers to be called to rescue these children.

What does the Scripture say about leaving children without adequate adult supervision?

Proverbs 29:15 says: *"Punishment and correction make a child wise. If he is left to do as he pleases, he will disgrace his mother."*

Child Abuse Revision

Review the keywords and terms discussed in this chapter and complete the crossword puzzle below:

Across

2. Raising a child that is not one's own by birth
6. Leave a child on its own without intending to return
7. Hiding or failing to deal with abuse
9. The psychological and physiological transition from childhood to adulthood
11. Allowed by law
14. Taking a child across state borders
16. Regarding the anus
17. Strategy to solicit consent to sexual abuse
18. Texting sexually explicit messages
20. Adults sexually attracted to children
21. Flag a serious warning or sign of impending trouble
22. Causes one to feel bad about oneself

Down

1. To do with the internet
3.. To do with how you feel
4. The illegal transportation of children for sale
5. Take advantage of the vulnerable
8. To leave a child's basic needs unattended or cared for
10. Of a sexual nature regarding children
12. Forcing a child into sexual activity
13. Forcing or manipulating others
15. Forced anal penetration
16. Legally parenting a child that is not one's own by birth
19 To refuse to bond or associate with a child

6

Do You Have Family Problems?

LESSONS

1. Child Shifting
2. Sibling Families
3. Latchkey and Barrel Children
4. The Breakdown of Family Values

Child Shifting

God designed the family as the basic unit that holds society together. Without the family, there can be no society. We are all part of the family of humanity in that our common ancestors are Adam and Eve, our fore parents. We have the divine DNA of God, our Creator. We are one human race, not many races as many believe. Our cultures differentiate us as we live and behave in specific ways that make us stand out. Otherwise, we are all humans, displaying the unity of God's image and the diversity of His creativity. We are outstanding among all God's other creations because we are the only creation made in God's image.

Abnormalities in the Family

When we depart from the time-honoured principles God gave us for starting and managing a family unit/household, we create far-reaching consequences for ourselves, our children, and their future generations. These consequences have become cyclical over the generations and difficult to resolve. Below, we will discuss some of the family abnormalities that have occurred and can affect you as a teenager. We also refer to these issues as **dysfunctional family life**, as the family is not currently functioning properly in society.

Child Shifting

Sometimes **child shifting** happens when children do not have a settled or stable place to call home and are frequently moved from one place to another. The movement is sometimes from one home or household to another, or it can be from one family member to another, from one caregiver to another, or from one institution to another.

Child shifting hurts because of unstable home or living arrangements. It can affect such children physically and emotionally, resulting in behavioural problems. Such teenagers can become insecure as they lack the nurturing they should have been given. They can experience depression, loneliness, anxiety/worry/fear as to where they will be going next and how they will be treated, especially if they had a bad experience previously.

They sometimes have to change schools and churches and move away from friends, teachers, and communities they have grown accustomed to or attached to. Teenagers are sometimes sexually abused in the process as they are moved from home to home. Child shifting can even cause them to run away from home or to end up living with paedophiles, older men or other abusive people, or they can become drug addicts or prostitutes, among other things.

Be aware that child-shifting can also cause you to self-harm, live in constant trauma, and have recurring nightmares as a result of not having a stable home. The most common trauma as a result of child-shifting is homelessness when the teenagers run away. While some countries have made significant efforts to prevent homelessness among children, the problem persists in some countries.

Homelessness can impact different areas of teenagers' lives, including their physical and mental health, education, safety, and overall well-being, thus making them more prone to harm and danger. Homeless teenagers can become street children. (Please see Chapter 8, Lesson 3, The Street and Working Children, section.)

Sibling Families

Do you know that while some of you live with parents or other adults, some teenagers don't have this luxury? They have what is called **Sibling Families.** This is a family form where siblings (brothers and sisters) live together without their parents. In some countries, older siblings are left to care for younger ones because the parents do not live at home with them due to some of the following reasons:

- Abandonment of the children

- Employment of parents too far away from home to return every day
- Migration of parents overseas
- Parents leave to start new families
- The death of parents leaves the children and teenagers as orphans, and they have to take care of themselves.

Sibling families can hurt the children because of the added pressure placed upon them as a family, especially the older ones who are themselves children. The younger ones also may lack the mature care an adult would provide for them.

Latchkey and Barrel Children

Key Term

Latchkey Children are those whose parents expect to operate independently and care for themselves without adult supervision for short periods daily. They are usually 'key carriers', where they may collect the house key

from neighbours or other adults or hidden places around the home when they leave school. They may even take the key to school if they are the last to leave home and the first to get home. The absence of adult supervision for portions of the day makes such children and teenagers vulnerable to various forms of abuse. Some of these children may live in communities where there are predators (someone who can sexually abuse them) lurking around to exploit them, knowing that there are no adults at home for a while.

In some communities, in Jamaica and South America, for example, there are **'Dons'** who are informal area or community leaders who usually control drugs or other illicit, business or criminal activities. They wield power over the citizens without considering the law. They sometimes prey on young girls by forcing them to be their sexual partners. Parents and guardians are helpless, fearful and angry due to the behaviours of the 'Dons.' When children are left by themselves, it opens the doors for them to be abused by 'Dons.'[1]

The presence of 'Dons' who can abuse children will also apply to all children left alone or unprotected, including barrel and latchkey children, sibling families, street and working children and other similar circumstances.

In addition to Latchkey Children, **Barrel Children** are left behind when their parents migrate overseas. They are usually left in the care of family members, friends, and neighbours or sometimes left alone for an older one to look after them. Barrel Children is the term used because the parents would send barrels or the equivalent from overseas with material things such as food, clothes, toys and other items for them. They also send money through remittances but are not physically present in the home. The children lack the physical presence, emotional care, and nurturing from their parents and are therefore not given the support they need to develop wholesomely. These children can be open to various types of abuse.

Here is a quiz for you.

Who are barrel children?

a. Children who roll a barrel down a hill
b. Children who store their clothes in a barrel
c. Children who carry drinking water to fill up a barrel

d. Children whose parents live overseas and send clothes, toys, money and other things

The Changing Roles of Women and Men

Values refer to beliefs, principles, and standards that we consider highly important or hold in high regard. These principles or standards will shape the society we want for ourselves and future generations. God has given us biblical values to guide us in managing our households.

Christian men and women should play their part in managing the affairs of the family and the home so that God is pleased. Throughout the ages, men and women performed different roles, ensuring the family is cared for. Women

were traditionally socialised to be in the private sphere or the home. They are natural nurturers who used to stay home and look after the family. Men were socialised to be in the public space and go out and work to take care of the family. Over the years, the roles of men and women have changed as more women entered the world of work.

As a result, there has been a considerable departure from traditional family values, which has impacted contemporary society. The roles of men and women have been changed in positive and negative ways. We will discuss how the family is coping since the **changing roles of women and men** have occurred.

Key Term

More women have engaged in careers over the last few decades than ever before. Men have also entered new roles, such as working in non-traditional areas of work, and some have even taken on the nurturing role within the home. As women work outside the home, there is a positive side as women's employment benefits their families as some contribute significantly or are the primary breadwinners. More women feel a sense of satisfaction and higher self-esteem while pursuing careers. According to Michelle Hon in the article THE CHILL

MOM,[2] she indicated that working moms can have positive effects on their children as they raise more independent children and inculcate in them self-esteem and hard work.

On the negative side, some children are either neglected, rejected, have to care for themselves, or are cared for by siblings or caregivers. These caregivers may be unable to provide the nurturing necessary and pass on the correct values to the children. For example, in many cases, a mother who would have had the choice to stay at home and breastfeed until the child is naturally weaned between 9 months to a year on average has to return to work after six weeks to 3 months, depending on the maternity laws or the pressure that exists to return to work. She, therefore, has less time to spend with the family, including children.

Also, some fathers are absent from the home and do not necessarily share in the nurturing role, so the children suffer because of their working mothers and absent fathers. Homes where either one or both parents are absent can deprive children of the care necessary for proper growth and development. Such children can experience hurt, pain and anguish from the lack of parental care.

What does the Bible say about the above situations:

Proverbs 11:29 says: *"Whoever brings trouble to his family will be left with nothing but the wind. And a foolish person will become a servant to the wise."*

Proverbs 24:3-4 says, *"3 It takes wisdom to have a good family. It takes understanding to make it strong. 4 It takes knowledge to fill a home with rare and beautiful treasures."*

With my dad in the military and my mother terminally ill, I was moved to several family members' homes before I was 10. Now, I know that's called child shifting.

Yeah, I also realised that I was a latchkey child. My parents went to work early and came home late, and I had to let myself into the house after school.

Let's complete this Crossword puzzle below to test our learning.

To help you recap the key points and terms learned in this chapter, complete the crossword puzzle:

Changes in the Family

Across

5. How things have been done for generations

7. Remittances sent from abroad to maintain children.

9. Assigned duties and responsibilities

10. Everyone and everything within the home as a unit

Down

1. Powerful self-appointed leaders who enforce their rule

2. People sharing common ancestors or blood ties

3. Blood-related brothers and sisters

4. Movement of people from one geographic location/place to another

6. beliefs that shape our decision-making

8. Children who are responsible for letting themselves in and out of the house

NOTES

7

Dealing With Your Problems in the Wrong Way

LESSONS

1. Substance Abuse
2. Social Media
3. Harmful Images, Information and Songs
4. Self-harming

Substance Abuse

Key Term

Very often, if you are a victim of abuse, you may become overwhelmed and find it difficult to cope. Typically, you may fall into a pattern of **Addictive Behaviours** to deal with your problems. These actions are habit-forming to the point of dependency in the case of substance abuse, compulsive in the case of gambling, and compelling in the case of pornography. You have lost your natural ability to exercise self-control and so behave compulsively. These are

unhealthy ways of handling your problems, and you should seek counselling immediately if you identify with any of the behaviours that we discuss in this chapter.

Substance Abuse

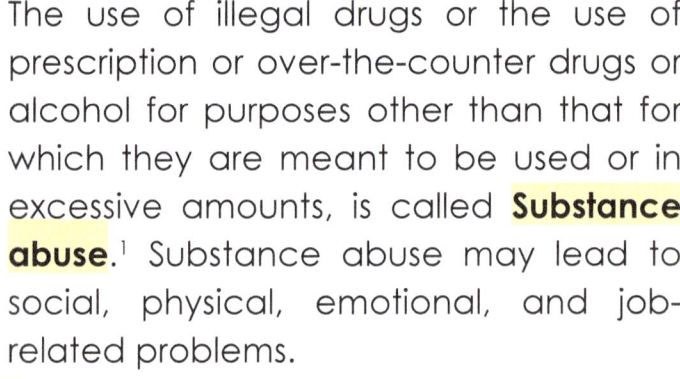

The use of illegal drugs or the use of prescription or over-the-counter drugs or alcohol for purposes other than that for which they are meant to be used or in excessive amounts, is called **Substance abuse**.[1] Substance abuse may lead to social, physical, emotional, and job-related problems.

So many things can happen to you in life. In addition to the abuses or harmful practices mentioned above, adults hurt you when they give you **drugs,** ask you to sell drugs or expose you to drugs such as ganja/marijuana, cocaine, crack, cigarettes, heroin, crystal meth, alcohol, 'molly' or other types of drugs. Sometimes, adults put drugs in sweets and drinks for sale to children. When they eat these items, they become addicted to the drugs. You are to stay away from these people and these substances.

Please see below the snippet from an article by ***The Recovery Village*** concerning drugs commonly used by teens.

> THE RECOVERY VILLAGE
>
> Drugs Commonly Used by Teens
>
> Editor Megan Hull
>
> Article at a Glance:
>
> - Teens often use drugs and alcohol to fit in or to cope with mental health issues, such as depression.
> - Teens may use substances to get feelings of temporary happiness and pleasure.
> - Commonly used drugs by teens are marijuana, cocaine, stimulants, and painkillers.
> - Teens also use K2, heroin, crystal meth, MDMA, hallucinogens, DXM, and inhalants.
> - The Recovery Village can help if your teen needs treatment for drug abuse.[2]

Key Words

As teenagers, you should not inhale or sniff **chemicals** or **substances** such as glue, gasoline, paint, paint thinners, shoe polish or similar substances to make you 'feel high' or to get temporary happiness and pleasure. This is harmful to you.

Inhaling the substances mentioned above is a type of drug abuse, and it can

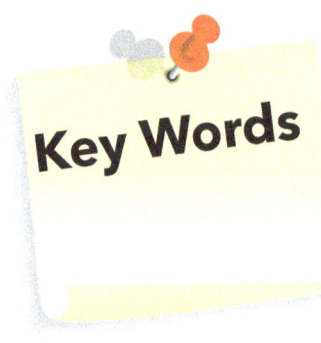

hurt you physically and emotionally after prolonged use. Using **inhalants** can lead to sexual abuse as well because you can lose control of yourself, awareness of your surroundings, and a sense of who you are and who you are with.

Vaping is also bad for you because it can lead to nicotine **addiction** and an increased risk of addiction to other drugs. Vaping is the inhaling of mist created by an electronic cigarette (e-cigarette). Vaping is seen as an alternative to smoking, but it can be equally dangerous. It is unfortunate that substances like vapes, products like cigars and cigarettes, and alcohol, among others, are readily available for purchase in stores. These Industries make millions selling products that are harmful as they have the potential to be addictive. You are safest avoiding them altogether so you do not have to enter the fight for freedom from substance abuse, which can be a life-long or lifetime activity.

Irresponsible Adult Behaviour

Sometimes, adults use drugs in your presence or ask you to purchase drugs for them. This is also wrong and is a form of abuse. When you are exposed to drugs, you must report the matter to a responsible adult whom you trust. These substances will ruin your physical and emotional health and even kill you.

Sometimes, children suffer when their parents use drugs or traffic drugs. When the parents are caught and imprisoned, the children suffer because they lack the care of the parents and are now vulnerable to various types of abuse in addition to their own physical and emotional anguish. Children like these are likely to end up in State care.

Digital Media Use

Key Term

As stated earlier in Chapter 2, Gen Z is the generation with access to various forms of digital devices. These digital devices expose them to more significant risks of digital abuse than previous generations. Some teenagers love to use **digital media**, the most popular type being the internet and social media. So much helpful information is available in this way. Did you know the *internet, social media,*

or other digital media can be good or bad for you? One positive way you can use the internet is to research for school assignments, learn more about different subjects, talk to your friends, or play games alone or with others. However, adults can use it to harm you. They can use it to get personal information about you, such as your address and phone numbers. Paedophiles can use the internet to communicate with you as well as, traffickers, sexual groomers, or other perverted persons. They can use information from the internet to find you and harm you. They are usually 'sweet talkers' who use manipulation to get you to do what they want. These predators can encourage you to call them or meet them at a private place, which is dangerous and harmful. Sometimes, children and teenagers are encouraged to run away from home to be with these predators, or they might want you to steal to help them. You should not do it!!

Paedophiles can enslave you and keep you locked away in some secret place for days, weeks, months or years so that your parents and the authorities cannot find you despite search efforts. It is not unusual to read about missing children who are found years later, sometimes alive or sometimes their dead bodies are found in woods, lakes or graves. Predators once took these children captive. As teenagers, you must avoid dangerous websites to protect yourself, so talk to your parents and guardians if you notice anything unusual when visiting websites. Various software and apps are available on the market to protect you as you browse the internet.

You must respect the rules for internet use when they are set in your home. You should be monitored when using the internet, watching videos or playing games because some of them may be harmful, and you may not know it. Do not be upset if your parents or guardians restrict the internet in a healthy way. It is for your safety and protection. They need to know if the materials you are exposed to can cause you harm. If something pops up on your computer screen or phone and you feel that it is harmful, you should report it to a responsible adult immediately. This site needs to be blocked and reported for your good.

Parents, guardians and other caregivers should be able to see the persons you are in contact with on the internet. They should also be able to examine the content you are reading, watching, or listening to. They should also be able to observe the conduct of the persons you associate with and the type of engagement you have with these persons you meet online or are online with. If these online persons tell you their connection with you should be kept a secret, this is a 'red flag' that something is wrong. ==Immediately tell your parents or guardians, who will provide further guidance.==

Avoid **'sexting'**, a word used to refer to a combination of sexual and texting. It is the act of sending sexual text messages. It often also involves pornographic messages and or sexual coding. Some parents may not understand 'sexting' and so may not be aware of the dangers you are exposed to when 'sexting.'

Please note that paedophiles, drug pushers, traffickers of children, serial killers, and psychopaths have total disregard for the law and manipulate and use people and social media as a means to lure you into their traps. ==Don't be naive; open your eyes and be wise!==

Harmful Images, Information and Songs

In addition to internet use, some books are good and provide helpful information. However, some adults write **harmful books** for you to read, which, for example, can teach you to commit crimes such as stealing. Sometimes, perverts want you to play **harmful games** or watch **harmful videos or movies** with them. These may contain sexual acts or x-rated information.

There are also **harmful songs** which can contain violence, expletives or explicit sexual expressions, or they may not be morally uplifting. They are designed to neutralise you against evil and wicked practices. You should avoid them. Some cartoons can desensitise small children and teenagers to pain and violence and can produce fear or aggression in them after they watch them.

Some of the harmful content to look out for includes:

Witchcraft/black and white magic/spell-casting/voodoo/obeah. This can introduce teenagers to practices that can cause demonic spirits to enter into or influence their lives. Sometimes, teenagers are killed through these ritualistic practices.

A report from an article posted by The Guardian Post in 2019 indicated that "Witchcraft and black magic are increasingly factors in the abuse of children, councils have warned, with official data showing child protection cases based on faith or belief are up by a third in the last year in England to almost 2,000. But there was also alarm that the numbers are rising so long after the high profile deaths of Victoria Climbié, eight, who was killed as a result of ritual abuse by her guardian in 2000, Khyra Ishaq, seven, who was starved to death in 2008 in Birmingham by her mother and her partner who had a strong belief in spirits and Kristy Bamu, 15, in 2010 killed by his sister and her partner in an exorcism in their east London flat".[3]

Undoubtedly there are many other incidents that could have taken place in other countries as well.

Here is a list of more harmful content

- Mediums/psychics, tarot card reading, and channelling can elicit actions similar to those reported by the Guardian Post above.
- Pornography, promiscuity, infidelity/cheating.
- Video games that promote violence, murder, robbery, drug use, expletives, disrespect and lawlessness among other things.
- Scamming/gambling. This can lead to addiction to gambling, which can lead to financial problems for teens. It can also lead to stealing from others, stress and anxiety issues.
- Some books, videos, movies, songs and games are not family-friendly or age-appropriate. Some feed children with a daily dose of violence. Some content will corrupt your mind, causing you to process information you are not emotionally mature enough to handle, hurting you. You may experience trauma, insomnia and nightmares or want to carry out these suggestive acts mentioned in these materials viewed, listened to or read. There have been cases in the news where children

have acted on content viewed and committed crimes or have come close. This is concerning; look at the article below.

Teens and social media use: What's the impact?

By Mayo Clinic Staff

How teens use social media might also determine its impact. For instance, viewing certain types of content may raise some teens' mental health risks. This could include content that depicts:

- Illegal acts.
- Self-harm or harm to other people.
- Encouragement of habits tied to eating disorders, such as purging or restrictive eating.[4]

In 2018, CNBC posted an article written by Josephine Bila entitled: **YouTube's Dark Side Could be Affecting Your Child's Mental Health.**

It listed the following points:

- Mental health experts warn that fear-inducing videos affect brain

> development in young children.
> • YouTube is toughening its approach to policing content for children. With 400 hours of video uploaded to YouTube every minute, vetting malicious content is proving difficult.
> • The American Academy of Paediatrics warns parents about the importance of limiting screen time.[5]

Harmful Images, Information & songs

Child pornography is any visual or picture of sexual conduct which can include sexually abusive images. As teenagers, you should not be exposed to pornographic materials in any form (audio or visual), which can be in print, electronic or digital. This is a type of child sexual abuse. This is harmful to you. You must report any exposure of this to a responsible adult. It can become addictive. Later on in life, you may find it difficult to establish a healthy, intimate relationship with the opposite sex when you get married.

Pornography can be in digital or print format. In fact, today, even adverts and commercials can be sexually explicit and leave unhealthy messages in your mind. You have the choice to switch off, swipe, block or delete such content from your gadget/device; don't get carried along with the popular wave of sexually explicit content.

==If you are ever contacted by anyone soliciting you to send them nude or sexually suggestive pictures of yourself or if they are offering to show you the same, this is a red flag that you are in danger. Immediately BLOCK them and report the incident to your parents or guardian. This is a matter for the police and should be treated seriously.==

The perpetrators mentioned above stalk and monitor teens with the intent to groom them into compliance with their sexually deviant intentions and use their images to make money. Your photos would end up on pornographic sites worldwide.

Teenagers Who Self-harm

In addition to harm inflicted on children

by parents, caregivers, family members, members of the school community, church members, community members, strangers and others, children also **self-harm**. They self-harm by inflicting pain on themselves as a coping mechanism due to some underlying problem such as trauma, pain and hurt that they perceive is caused by others.

Self-harm can also lead to suicide. Self-harm can manifest in unexplained physical injuries such as bruises, cuts, burns, bite marks, and body mutilation, among other things. It can also manifest itself in emotional ways, such as isolation from friends and families, moodiness, self-blame, and angry outbursts, among other things.

If you feel that you want to harm yourself, do not be afraid to tell your parents or guardians, a Guidance Counsellor or a trusted adult who can get you the necessary help.

According to the American Academy of Adolescent Psychiatry, suicides among young people continue to be a serious problem. Suicide is the second leading cause of death for children, adolescents, and young adults aged 15 to 24 year olds.

The majority of children and adolescents who attempt suicide have a significant mental health disorder, usually depression.

Among teenagers, suicide attempts may be associated with feelings of stress, self-doubt, pressure to succeed, financial uncertainty, disappointment, and loss. For some teens, suicide may appear to be a solution to their problems.[6]

Let's Test our Learning

1. Please tick the one that best describes child drug abuse.

    a. Adults giving a child Marijuana to smoke
    b. A child passing a shop where cigarettes are sold
    c. A child watching someone smoke a cigarette on TV
    d. School children watching a drunken man on the street

2. Search the chapter above and place a definition that matches each keyword or statement provided until all are completed.

3. Also, complete the following: What name is given to the statements below:

    a. Electronic communication _____

    b. Adults who satisfy their sexual urges with children_____

4. Y/N is vaping or cigarettes substance abuse?_____

The Lord Jesus does not want you to abuse your body, and neither does He want anyone to abuse you.

Here is what the Scriptures say about abusing your body.

1 Corinthians 6:19-20 says:

"You should know that your body is a temple for the Holy Spirit. The Holy Spirit is in you. You have received the Holy Spirit from God. You do not own yourselves. You were bought by God for a price. So honour God with your bodies."

141 Love Me Don't Hurt Me

1. Substance abuse
   _____
2. Witchcraft
   _____
3. Illicit Drugs
   _____
4. Harmful Chemicals
   _____
5. Sexting
   _____
6. Pornography
   _____
7. Self Harm
   _____

I was hooked on pornography once; I still struggle, but now I know the consequences. I am seeing a counsellor. I want to stop completely.

I tried smoking marijuana, even though I knew it was substance abuse. It made me tired and uncoordinated, and my performance at football was terrible. It's not for me.

NOTES

8

Are You a Vulnerable Teenager?

LESSONS

1. Children with Disabilities

2. Children in State Care

3. Street and Working Children

4. Teen Prostitution

Children with Disabilities

Key Word

Did you know that **Children with Disabilities** are <mark>vulnerable</mark> because they may not be fully able-bodied or able-minded due to some birth defect or an accident later on? Therefore, disabilities can be physical [lacking the full use of your body] or mental [lacking the ability to reason].

If you have a disability, you are to be loved, respected and cared for like

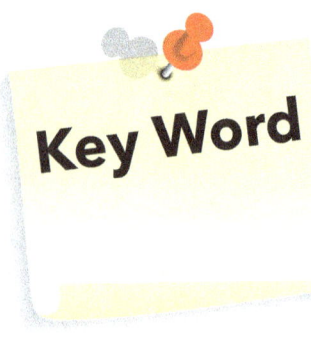

anyone else. You should not be mocked, laughed at, jeered, made fun of, or **discriminated** against. When this happens, it hurts you. You should be given the same rights and privileges as children who are fully able-bodied. You are just as precious as anyone else. You may sometimes be disadvantaged and made vulnerable, but in God's view, you must always be protected.

What Provisions Are to be Place for The Disabled?

Special provisions should be made to help people with various types of disabilities. Some of these provisions should include buildings, public spaces, and transportation retrofitted for easy access (wheelchair or otherwise). These include uncluttered sidewalks, ramps, stair lifts, guard rails, access to jobs, access to education and training facilities, access to health programmes, tools and equipment that can assist their disabilities, among other things.

Some countries have laws governing how persons with disabilities are to be treated. These laws must be enforced to prevent hurt to children with disabilities, teenagers and persons in general who have disabilities.

How does the Bible say that a person with a disability is to be treated?

Leviticus 19:14 says: *"You must not curse a deaf man. And you must not put something in front of a blind person to make him fall. But you must respect your God. I am the Lord."*

Are you surprised that the Bible has laws for the treatment of the disabled? Why do you think it says you must respect the Lord in the scripture above?

_____
_____
_____
_____

How were disabled people in biblical times treated according to the scripture above? Did God approve of their behaviour?

_____
_____
_____
_____

Psalm 146:8 says: *"The Lord gives sight to the blind."*

There are several cases where Jesus healed children who were sick or disabled, as found in the scriptures below:-

The Epileptic Boy - Matthew 17:14-18

'14 Jesus and his followers went back to the crowd. A man came to Jesus and bowed before him.
15 The man said, "Lord, please help my son. He has epilepsy and is suffering very much. He often falls into the fire or into the water.
16 I brought him to your followers, but they could not cure him."
17 Jesus answered, "You people have no faith. Your lives are all wrong. How long must I stay with you? How long must I continue to be patient with you? Bring the boy here."
18 Jesus gave a strong command to the demon inside the boy. Then the demon came out, and the boy was healed.'

The Dying Boy - St. John 4:46-53

'46 Jesus went to visit Cana in Galilee again. This is where Jesus had changed the water into wine. One of the king's important officers lived in the city of Capernaum. This man's son was sick.
47 The man heard that Jesus had come from Judea and was now in Galilee. He went to Jesus and begged him to come

to Capernaum and heal his son. His son was almost dead.

48 Jesus said to him, "You people must see signs and miracles before you will believe in me."

49 The officer said, "Sir, come before my child dies."

50 Jesus answered, "Go! Your son will live."

The man believed what Jesus told him and went home.

51 On the way, the man's servants came and met him. They told him, "Your son is well."

52 The man asked, "What time did my son begin to get well?"

They answered, "It was about one o'clock yesterday when the fever left him."

53 The father knew that one o'clock was the exact time that Jesus had said, "Your son will live." So, the man and all the people of his house believed in Jesus.'

The Dead Girl - St Matthew 9:18, 23-25

'18 While Jesus was saying these things, a ruler of the synagogue came to him. The ruler bowed down before Jesus and said, "My daughter has just died. But come and touch her with your hand, and she will live again…"

23 Jesus continued along with the ruler and went into the ruler's house. Jesus saw people there who play music for funerals. And he saw many people there crying.
24 Jesus said, "Go away. The girl is not dead. She is only asleep." But the people laughed at Jesus.
25 After the crowd had been put outside, Jesus went into the girl's room. He took her hand, and she stood up.'

When children with disabilities are treated badly, this type of behaviour displeases God. When you disrespect people with disabilities, you are disrespecting God. Jesus demonstrated compassion towards all the children in the Bible whom He healed from sickness or disabilities. This is an example for us to follow.

Matthew 18:10 *"Jesus said, 'Be careful. Don't think these little children are worth nothing. I tell you that they have angels in heaven who are always with my Father in heaven.'"*

Write some instances where you have seen a disabled person being protected/abused in your community.

_____

_____

_____
_____
_____

Children in State Care

Do you know that some teenagers do not live in a home with their parents for various reasons? These teenagers live in **children's homes/orphanages, places of safety, state care/ government homes and remand centres.**

A **Children's Home or State or Government Home** is where children and teenagers don't live with their families but live together, where professionals (child protection officers, counsellors, and career professionals) look after them. The government or the State can run these Homes. Some of these children are orphans because both parents are dead due to illnesses. In some countries, children become orphans because their

Key Word

parents die from HIV/AIDS, or some parents are victims of war and conflicts. Some have been abandoned, rejected or neglected by parents and other family members who are unable to take care of them. Children in these homes should get the same love, care and access to resources from caregivers. You should not be hurt or mistreated if you are in one of these homes.

A **Place of Safety** is a temporary government home for children between ages eight and 18 awaiting court decisions and others who conflict with the law or have behavioural problems.

What does the Bible Say?

James 1:27 *"Religion that God our Father accepts as pure and faultless is this: to look after orphans and widows in their distress and to keep oneself from being polluted by the world."*

John 14:18 *"I will not leave you all alone like orphans. I will come back to you."*

What do these two scriptures tell you about God's heart towards orphaned and abandoned children?

_____

Street And Working Children

Again, teenagers and some children do not have what is considered a stable home or a home where the necessities are provided. They form part of the vulnerable, high-risk group called **street children.** They fall into the three categories mentioned below:-

1. <u>Children of the street</u> who live and work there (selling, begging, making a living on the street without adult supervision).

2. <u>Children on the street</u> who, during the day, beg, sell items, or try to make a living but go home at night to sleep.

3. <u>Children who live on the street</u> with their families because they are homeless.

Do you know that no child of a certain age should be on the street begging or working to provide for themselves? Adequate facilities should be available to

Key Term

protect children at a certain age based on the laws in your country. For example, in Jamaica, based on the law, **Child Labour** should only be allowed if it is light work for children ages 13-16. Children under the age of 13 should not be employed. Children should not be engaged in dangerous forms of child labour, like deep sea diving for money, handling hazardous substances, and exposure to sexual exploitation.

Some children in some countries and communities are not allowed to go to school on a Friday because they have to assist on the farm, sell in the market or on the streets or perform other income-generating activities. Such responsibilities disrupt a child's education and can harm the child. Children who are engaged in such activities are considered Child Labourers. No child or teenager should have to beg for food or to provide necessities for themselves, but the reality is some of them have to do so based on their circumstances. Poverty is at the heart of Child Labour.

According to UNICEF, *'nearly 1 in 10 children are subjected to child labour worldwide, with some forced into hazardous work through trafficking'*.[1]

Chapter 8 | Are You a Vulnerable Teenager?

Do you know the child labour law in your country? Please research and write it below.

_____
_____
_____

Draw a straight line from the abuse to the matching example of abuse.

Abuse

- Elder abuse
- Spousal abuse
- Sibling violence

Examples of abuse

- When mom and dad fight
- When brother and sister fight
- Talking down to your grandparents

I mocked a disabled girl once, but now I know that it is wrong.

I cursed a street child for begging, but I feel awful now that I know it is wrong.

9

Do You Feel Safe and Secure?

LESSONS

1. Violence in the Home
2. Violence in Communities
3. Violence in Schools

Chapter 9 | Do You Feel Safe and Secure?

Violence in the Home

Key Term

The Home is a place where teenagers should feel safe. Still, some teenagers witness or experience **domestic violence** or violence in the home that occurs amongst persons that are related by blood, law or intimacy. They witness or experience sibling abuse, elder abuse, child abuse and spousal or intimate partner violence, which can be physical,

emotional, sexual, financial, or spiritual, among other things.

Sibling abuse is the intentional physical, emotional or sexual harm done by one sibling to another. It is a form of power and control where one sibling tries to exercise authority over another. It can be brother to brother, sister to sister, brother to sister or sister to brother. This form of violence sometimes happens when you get in a quarrel or fight with your siblings over room space, possessions, or even parental love. Sometimes, it is a win-lose situation because someone ends up being hurt. It is best to settle disputes in an amicable way to avoid this kind of violence. Get in the habit of talking things out calmly in a timely manner. Don't allow grievances or misunderstandings to go unresolved, letting them simmer until they spill over into negative communication, which often leads to violent reactions from the insulted or angry party.

Elders are considered adults over 60 years of age. When it comes to **elder abuse,** anybody within the home can abuse older adults. Still, as teenagers, you can abuse older adults by inflicting intentional harm or neglecting those who are over 60 years of age. Sometimes, teenagers emotionally abuse older adults when they speak unkindly to them. Sometimes, they get physical, too, by hitting or slapping the older adult. Sometimes, they also abuse them financially by defrauding them of their possessions. All these types of abuses, although inflicted on older adults, can also hurt you because they can put a barrier between you and your elderly relatives. It can also prevent the transfer of inter-generational wealth, values and wisdom.

Spousal abuse or intimate partner violence occurs amongst those who are related by intimacy or law. It involves physical harm such as hitting, beating and sometimes the use of weapons. It can also involve emotional harm where there is name-calling, belittling and other such acts. It can also involve sexual harm, where they are forced into unwanted sexual acts by the other partner. When these acts take place, they can lead to divorce and separation of parents.

Spousal abuse can hurt teenagers because they get caught in the crossfire of the toxic relationship that exists between parents or family members who are in intimate relationships.

Effects of Spousal Abuse on Teenagers

This can have traumatic effects on the children who experience violence in the home. One of the effects that family violence or spousal or intimate partner violence can have on children is that you can be injured physically during this violent blow-up.

You can also suffer emotionally from feelings of fear, guilt, anger, helplessness, or resentment towards one or both parents. It can also cause you to have sleepless nights, develop poor eating habits, run away from home, under-perform in school or force you to seek help in the wrong places. Constant exposure to this type of violence in the home can cause you to be desensitised to violence, which may cause you to believe it is normal. Spousal abuse can also affect your relationships when you are seeking a partner to marry.

Chapter 9 | Do You Feel Safe and Secure? **160**

Violence in Communities

Do you know that sometimes children who live in certain countries and communities are exposed to violence due to political wars, gang warfare, drug dealings and killings, robbery or shooting, among other things? Some children are more exposed than others to **community violence.** The extent is determined by the community or country in which you live. Children are sometimes physically, sexually and emotionally abused or killed in the process as they are caught in the crossfire. According to Learning English (October 2021), in Mexico, children as young as ten are recruited by Drug Cartels.[1]

In Jamaica, children, primarily teenagers, are both victims and perpetrators of gun crimes. Some of the perpetrators have been apprehended and brought before the law. Police Commissioner Major General Antony Anderson says that 875 major crimes committed in Jamaica from 2019 to 2022 were carried out by perpetrators between 15 and 17 years of age.[2]

On November 6, 2022, The Child Protection and Family Services Agency (CPFSA) noted that *"Hundreds of Jamaican children are being held hostages of gang violence, not only as homicide and trauma victims but also as innocent onlookers of their guardians' criminal and deadly deeds."*[3]

According to UNICEF, armed groups in Nigeria have recruited at least 8,000 boys and girls since 2009. Most of the recruitment took place by **Boko Haram**, which is an Islamic militant group based in Northeastern Nigeria. These children are used to fight other groups opposed to the Boko Haram regime. Children, mainly girls, were also used in suicide attacks. Over the years, several young girls have been kidnapped by the Islamic terrorist group Boko Haram in Nigeria.[4] Several schools have been targeted, where girls have been abducted, raped, killed, or forced into 'marriages.'[5] This hurts teens in every way.

According to the Convention on the Rights of the Child, when it comes to armed conflict, you have the right to

Chapter 9 | Do You Feel Safe and Secure? **162**

> The NetFlix film Beasts Of No Nation released in 2015, starring Edris Alba, depicts the experiences of children abducted and forced to be child soldiers.

protection and freedom from war. Children under 15 cannot be forced to go into the army or take part in war. ==This means that they should not be forced to become child soldiers.==

Can you find a film or documentary online that depicts the experiences of children abducted and forced to be child soldiers?

UNICEF further indicated that *'thousands of children are recruited and used in armed conflicts across the world. Between 2005 and 2022, more than 105,000 children were verified as recruited and used by parties to the conflict, although the actual number of cases is believed to be much higher.'*[6]

A UNICEF Report indicated that *' in his 2015 report on children and armed conflict, the United Nations Secretary-General indicates that 49 of the 57 parties to armed conflict that are listed as perpetrators of violations against children are non-State armed groups. For example, in Iraq and the Syrian Arab Republic, the proliferation of armed groups and the military advances by ISIL have made children even more vulnerable to recruitment. Children as young as age 12 are undergoing military training as well as being used as informants and guards at checkpoints and other strategic locations. Armed groups in other conflicts are also abducting children, including groups in Afghanistan, the Democratic Republic of the Congo, Nigeria, Somalia and South Sudan.'*[7]

As much as possible, your parents, guardians, community members, and government should ensure you have a safe environment to live in. Thousands of children were either killed, injured or had to flee their countries due to wars in the Middle East and Europe in recent times.

According to the United Nations, a record 37 million children are displaced as refugees worldwide (UNICEF). Migratory displacement due to war hurts children of all ages. Sometimes, children are separated from their parents, and some may never be reunited.

Refugees are people who have to flee their country of origin to another country because they do not feel protected there. This could be due to war, conflicts, and religious upheavals, among other things. They leave everything behind and may not be able to return to their country or are unwilling to return because of fear for their lives, or they may not have the necessary means to survive in their home country. Sometimes, they travel miles by land or sea to get away. Families sometimes make risky journeys by sea with their children as they flee their country.

Refugees need basic things to survive. Some die in the process of fleeing due to lack of food and water, malnutrition, illnesses, or exhaustion. Some even die due to emotional and physical stress, torture and extreme environmental conditions, among other things.

In addressing this situation, Governments should seek measures to protect you from harm and danger if you live in these countries and communities where you must flee to seek refugee status elsewhere. Very often, even if these children are not physically harmed, they are psychologically traumatised because they have witnessed so much violence and evil around them. Their studies are disrupted when they are too afraid and unsettled to learn. Refugees' health may also be compromised.

Violence In Schools

Since you spend most of your childhood life in schools, you should be protected from **violence within the school community.** In addition to community violence, schools are places where you can be exposed to harm.

School violence is perpetrated by one student to another, where some children take weapons, including guns, knives and other implements, to school. They sometimes fight and injure each other. This happens in some Caribbean countries, other countries and certainly in the United States of America (USA).

Key Term

In the USA, in addition to violence perpetrated by one student toward another, over the years, there have been several **mass shootings** where several children have been killed by attackers from within or outside the school community. The attackers go into the schools or are in the schools where they shoot and cause physical and or emotional injury to children, teachers and other staff, some of whom are injured or die during the attacks. Mass shootings are very traumatic and can have a long-lasting emotional effect on the school community, parents, and the community where the violence has taken place.

When it comes to School Violence, UNICEF has indicated the following:

- *'Globally, half of students aged 13–15, some 150 million – report experiencing peer-to-peer violence in and around school.*

- *Slightly more than 1 in 3 students between the ages of 13 and 15 experience bullying, and about the same proportion are involved in physical fights.*

- *Around 720 million school-aged children live in countries where they are not fully protected by law from corporal punishment at school.*

- *Between 2005 and 2020, the United Nations verified more than 13,900 incidents of attacks, including direct attacks or attacks where there has not been an adequate distinction between civilian and military objectives on educational and medical facilities and protected persons, including pupils and hospitalised children, and health and school personnel.'*[8]

Violence in any shape or form hurts children, including teenagers, as it affects all areas of their lives. It not only affects them in the home but also in schools and communities, even to the extent that some are injured or die in the process.

What do the Scriptures say about these situations? Here are two scriptures to show that the Lord cares about you.

Jeremiah 22:3 says:

"This is what the Lord says: Do what is fair and right. Protect those who have been robbed from those who robbed them. Don't do any wrong to the orphans or widows. Don't hurt them. Don't kill innocent people here."

Psalm 22:24 says:

"The Lord does not ignore the one who is in trouble. He doesn't hide from him. He listens when the one in trouble calls out to him."

God is Justice in the same way that He is love. It's His nature to be just, fair, and righteous. He has promised that He will

Chapter 9 | Do You Feel Safe and Secure? **168**

deliver us from all harm and ensure we receive justice when we are aggrieved. This is no less so for children and teenagers who are victims of armed conflicts within their community.

> A girl in my school who lived in a rough neighbourhood was caught in a school shooting between gangs. She prayed and escaped. Then her parents moved her to our school. It's a good thing they are Christians.

> My parents pray for me every morning before I leave for school. If I feel afraid, I repeat Psalm 91. It always calms me. I trust God.

Do you believe God keeps His promise to protect His children? God never promised that bad things won't happen to good people. He promised always to be present to help us. Complete the table below.

Scripture	Incident /person	God's response
Matthew 14	Peter was drowning.	Jesus reached out and lifted him to safety.
Which Scripture?	The King threw him into the lions' den for praying to God.	What did God do?
Acts 23	WHO?	God appeared and promised to save Him
Daniel 3:17-18	WHO/WHAT?	What did God do?

Psalm 34:19 says: *"People who do what is right may have many problems. But the Lord will solve them all."*

Let's test our learning.

1. Define the keywords/Key terms below.
    1. Domestic Violence
    2. Sibling Abuse
    3. Spousal Abuse
    4. Community Violence
    5. Mass Shootings
    6. Refugees
2. Choose two items from the list of abuses above. Write a scenario outlining how to avoid or reduce the risk of each type of abuse.
3. In the media, we often hear the term victim blame. We are challenged against blaming victims when abuse is reported and made public. What do you think about this term and how it is used?
4. Do you think that victims have any responsibility to protect themselves or can take action to prevent abuse?
5. Find one famous case of child abuse that was reported in the media in your country or internationally and examine the actions of the parents/adults in charge and the victims.

a. Say if the victims are to be blamed
b. Say if the parents are to be blamed
c. Was the incident of abuse unavoidable, given the circumstances?
d. If not, recommend some ways that it could have been prevented.

I have learnt so many things that I can do to prevent or reduce abuse. Praying for families experiencing domestic abuse is a starting point.

One of my takeaways from this lesson is that I must know the child helpline in my country to report abuse. It's happening even where you don't expect it.

10 Abuses Embedded in Cultural Traditions:

LESSONS

1. Child Marriage
2. Female Genital Mutilation
3. Period Poverty
4. Child Stealing
5. Teen Prostitution
6. Abortion
7. Sex Selection
8. Witchcraft, Cults and Occults

Chapter 10 | Abuses Embedded in Cultural Traditions **172**

Child Marriage

Did you ever imagine that there may be cultural practices that are considered types of abuse that can hurt you as a teenager, even though people may accept them in your society as being normal?

UNICEF indicated that **'harmful cultural practices'** pose another grave risk in various parts of the world. For example, hundreds of millions of girls have been subjected to child marriage and female genital mutilation – even though both are internationally recognised human rights

Key Term

violations.[1] Another cultural practice that hurts teenagers is **Child Marriage**, sometimes referred to as Child Brides - According to UNICEF, Child marriage refers to any formal marriage or informal union between a child under the age of 18 and an adult or another child.

Despite a steady decline in this harmful practice over the past decade, child marriage remains widespread, with approximately one in five girls married in childhood across the globe, as indicated by UNICEF.[2]

These children are forced into this situation and cannot enjoy their childhood. These are generally practices found in Eastern countries. Here are some statistics extracted from the World Vision Report concerning child brides. World Vision has indicated that 'according to the 2017 UNICEF report, *State of the World's Children*, the countries with the highest rates of child marriage before age 18 (counted among women now 20 to 24) are:

Countries With The Highest Rates Of Child Marriage Before Age 18 [3]

2017 UNICEF report

Country	Percentages
1. Niger -	76%
2. Central African Republic -	68%
3. Chad -	67%
4. Bangladesh -	59%
5. Mali -	52%
6. South Sudan -	52%
7. Burkina Faso -	52%
8. Guinea -	51%
9. Mozambique -	48%
10. India -	47%

Of the 25 countries with the highest rates of child marriage, almost all are affected by conflict, fragility, or natural disasters, World Vision reported.[4]

Female Genital Mutilation

Female Genital Mutilation (FGM) is a type of child abuse which refers to 'all procedures involving partial or total removal of the female external genitalia or other injury to the female genital organs for non-medical reasons.' (UNICEF's definition).

It is most often carried out on young girls between infancy and age 15. In every form in which it is practised, FGM is a violation of girls' and women's fundamental human rights, including their rights to health, security and dignity. According to UNFPA (United Nations Population Fund), it estimates 68 million girls are at risk of being mutilated between 2015 and 2030. A more recent study estimates an additional two million girls to be at risk of this harmful practice due to COVID-19. Protecting girls will take a significant push to accelerate the elimination of this harmful, often deadly, practice.[5]

UNFPA further reported that the practice of FGM is evidenced in some countries in Africa, Asia, the Middle East, and Eastern Europe to a lesser extent. FGM is presently practised in the diaspora communities that reside in South America and Western countries where diaspora populations reside.

Period Poverty

Poverty affects both teenage boys and girls, but sometimes in different ways. **Period Poverty**[6] is one thing that only affects women and girls of menstrual age in a negative way in developed, middle and low-income countries.

Some teenage girls who experience period poverty can suffer from deep physical and emotional health. Period Poverty happens when teenagers cannot afford to purchase sanitary napkins or products for use during menstruation due to poverty; they are forced to use unsafe products, thus harming their health. Going without adequate sanitary pads increases their

risk of infection and other health issues.

According to the National Library of Medicine and the National Center for Biotechnology Information, Period Poverty is the lack of access to safe and hygienic menstrual products during monthly periods and inaccessibility to basic sanitation services or facilities and menstrual hygiene education.

"It has been proven that many countries are still affected by the period stigma and taboo, inadequate exposure to menstrual health and its management, lack of education about menstruation, and shortage of access to menstrual products and facilities." [7]

Child Stealing

Child stealing happens when a child is taken/abducted, kidnapped or hidden from parents or legal guardians or persons having custody of the child. Children are sometimes stolen from parks, malls, hospitals and homes for various reasons, including for purposes of

Chapter 10 | Abuses Embedded in Cultural Traditions 178

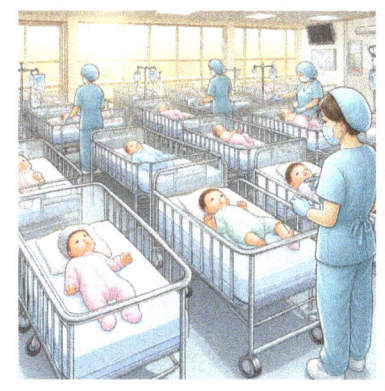

trafficking or to be used by paedophiles. Also many families that do not have children especially women who are childless and pressured by their spouses or the communities in which they live to have a child at all cost.

One parent will steal their child/children from the other parent who has legal custody. All these actions hurt children. Often, twins and children of other multiple births are keen targets of child stealing, especially from hospitals or children's homes.

Child abduction or child theft hurts children. According to Wikipedia, *Child Abduction* or child theft is *"the unauthorised removal of a minor (a child under the age of legal adulthood) from the custody of the child's natural parents or legally appointed guardians."*[8]

The term 'child abduction' includes two legal and social categories which differ by the method of abduction:

1. Abduction by members of the child's family or 2. Abduction by strangers.

Parental/family child abduction is the unauthorised custody of a child by usually one parent without parental agreement between both parents and contrary to

family law ruling, which may have removed the child from the care, access and contact of the other parent and family side. This is the most common form of child abduction, and it happens during parental separation or divorce. The bias is usually on the father's side in Eastern cultures and on the mother's side in Western cultures. In either case, child abduction hurts these children, who may be alienated or disconnected from one side of the family.

Abduction or kidnapping by strangers by people unknown to the child and outside the child's family also takes place. A stranger might kidnap a child for extortion/ransom from the parents for the child's return.

Sometimes, children are stolen as part of the human trafficking ring to exploit them through slavery, forced labour, or sexual abuse. Prostitution of these children/teenagers is very high on the list of traffickers.

Teen Prostitution

Forced Child Prostitution

Forced Child prostitution is present in several countries across the globe. It is a serious human rights issue and a cause for health concern among children. Teenagers of all ages can be forced into prostitution. As the economic situation gets worse, families force their children into harmful sexual practices such as prostitution.

This is a practice that hurts teenagers as it can cause girls and boys of all ages to be physically, emotionally and sexually abused. Forced **Child Prostitution** is when children are forced into sexual activities in exchange for money or material gain. Most of the time, it is with older men. Sometimes, parents or other family members force their children into prostitution to get financial gain as a means of addressing their economic needs. Also connected to child prostitution are abusive cultural practices and gender discrimination. Girls are mainly the ones forced into prostitution, but boys can also be forced, given the high demand for sex from both males and females.

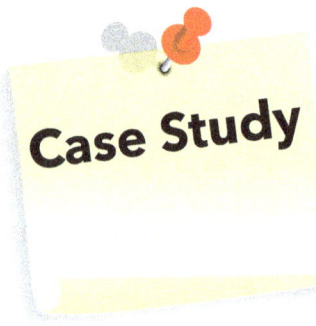

In the Case of Jamaica - Here is a snippet from an online article published in Jamaica on Friday, February 27, 2015, in The Gleaner:

"Almost one year after the St Thomas police raised the red flag about parents in the parish pushing their children into sexual activities in return for money, the problem is continuing with fresh concerns about the impact this is having on the children.

What I have seen is pimping of our children whereby families are unable to take care of themselves economically, so the children are given the responsibility of bringing in money to the family," Lorian Peart-Roberts of the Social Development Commission (SDC) in St Thomas told a Gleaner Editors' Forum last Thursday."

'The girls especially are foisted on men of better means, and they are expected to support the family. It is not a guessing game and a widespread problem across the parish of St Thomas," added Peart-Roberts."[9]

Chapter 10 | Abuses Embedded in Cultural Traditions 182

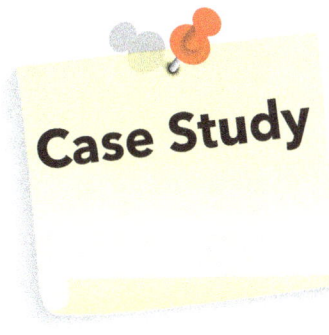

The above statement was made at a multi-agency empowerment session in the parish of St. Thomas to address the alarming problem of child sexual abuse.

In the Case of the Philippines - Here is a snippet of an article written by Ralph Jennings, posted online on December 04, 2020.

"Child prostitution is surging this year in the Philippines, where parents have lost jobs during strict anti-pandemic shutdowns and allowed their children to work the sex trade, often through online connections, activists and officials say.

Officials in the Southeast Asian country believe COVID-19 is fuelling an increase in online sexual exploitation of children, the government's Commission on Human Rights said in September. UNICEF had already described the Philippines four years ago as **"the global epicentre of the live-stream sexual abuse trade."**

International advocacy group **End Child Prostitution and Trafficking** *estimates a 264% increase in online sexual abuse and exploitation of children during the pandemic, the domestic news website Manila Bulletin reports. Child prostitution is happening largely at home, often* *involving fathers, stepfathers, uncles or older brothers, Dela Rosa said. Now, adults in the family are helping their children use the internet to set up paid sex with people from outside the home, a source of family income, she said. She added that the internet's prevalence facilitates advertising, finding customers and getting paid."*[10]

In the Case of India - Here is a snippet from a blog entitled CHILD PROSTITUTION IN INDIA, posted by Admin in the Journal of Legal Research and Judicial Sciences (JLRJS).

"Child Sexual Commercial Exploitation is a big problem in India. The group of traffickers kidnap the girls from the road, market, and mall and sell them to brothels and the international flesh trade; sometimes, their parents force them to enter this field because of poverty and lack of education.

These girls and women are forced to be prostitutes in the Indian flesh trade on a plague level. The customers of the business abuse the girl daily and treat her like a commodity. Girls traffic from Nepal and Bangladesh sell them in Indian brothel houses, flesh trade, marriage, etc. This is very shameful for us.

*In this article, we will discuss the concept of **Child Prostitution Acts** implemented and the legal framework in India combating this crime. There are many acts enforced related to this problem, but these laws do not seem to be adequate or comprehensive in dealing with various forms of trafficking. We want more effective laws and amendments. There are a lot of cases on child prostitution pending in the Supreme Court. Victims face many problems like drug addiction and HIV/AIDS."*[11]

Imagine we have only briefly examined three cases and there are many, many more. Prostitution can leave children physically abused as their bodies can get torn and injured during the sexual activities. They are also at risk for teenage pregnancy, sexually transmitted disease, and other bodily injuries and even death. Emotionally, the children can suffer mental illness, post-traumatic stress disorder, sleep and eating disorders, guilt and shame, among a range of other issues. It also retards the educational and other developmental areas of children.

State the kinds of laws you think these countries need to put in place to stop teen prostitution.

Is there any cultural practice, bias, or belief that needs to be challenged or changed in the three case studies?

_____
_____
_____
_____

Abortion

Abortion is a voluntary termination of pregnancy for various reasons which kills the unborn child. This is a type of child abuse affecting the unborn child since it involves killing. Some scholarly articles suggest that when adolescents have abortions, it affects them as well. They can suffer from guilt, anger, shame, insomnia, nightmares about babies, among other things. Some abortions can lead to the death of the mothers as well.

Some countries have laws on abortion.

Research and indicate your country's laws, and write your findings below.

_____
_____

Discuss the alternatives to abortion for unplanned pregnancies.

_____
_____

What does the Scripture say about Abortion?

While the Bible does not use the word Abortion, there are Scripture references that point to the commencement of life being with God and that He sees, knows and cares for the unborn and has a plan for every human life. This is called **predestination.** Therefore, since He was intentional in creation, God considers life to be sacred/precious; this is called the **sanctity of life**. Here are three Scriptures:

Jeremiah 1:4-5 says:

'4 The Lord spoke these words to me
5 "Before I made you in your mother's womb, I chose you. Before you were

born, I set you apart for a special work. I appointed you as a prophet to the nations."'

If life begins at conception, then to take a life, whether by way of abortion or otherwise, is to commit murder, as indicated below:

Deuteronomy 27:25 says, '*Anyone will be cursed who takes money to murder an innocent person. Then all the people will say, "Amen!"*'

Advice for teenagers who have had abortions

It may be difficult to counsel a teen who had an abortion for whatever reason. As a teenager, you are not in a position to offer medical or professional advice, but if you or anyone you know has had an abortion, the following can be done:

1. Seek professional help where needed
2. Seek out trusted persons who can help build your self-esteem, as you may be suffering from shame, guilt, depression, or the pain of loss.
3. Ask the Lord for forgiveness and receive His forgiveness to help you walk free of guilt.
4. Know that - *"The Lord's love never ends. His mercies never stop. They are*

new every morning…" **Lamentations 3:22-33.**

5. Know that - *"… if we confess our sins, he will forgive our sins. We can trust God. He does what is right. He will make us clean from all the wrongs we have done."* **1 John 1:9**

Isaiah 49:1 says: *"All of you people in faraway places, listen to me. Listen, all you nations far away. Before I was born, the Lord called me to serve him. The Lord named me while I was still in my mother's body."*

Here are some Bible-based reasons to be PRO-LiFE. What is your view?

1. Babies have rights too.

2. Life begins in the womb.

3. Many people who can't have children want babies to adopt.

4. Every child has a God-given destiny for the Earth.

5. You shall not commit murder applies to abortion.

Sex Selection

One would think that when women get pregnant, they will give birth if no abortion or miscarriage takes place. This is not always the case, as in some cultures, children are sometimes selected to live or die based on their sex. This is called **Sex Selection.** This is done either before or after birth as parents exercise preference for one sex over another. The child who is not selected is rejected because it is not the preferred sex choice. Girls are often rejected when this decision is made. 'Son preference' is particularly strong in various countries, from North Africa, the Middle East, South Asia, and East Asia. The strongest preference for sons has been found in India, Nepal, Bangladesh, Egypt, South Korea, and China."[12]

Bacha posh is a practice in some countries like Afghanistan, where male status is important in some families. As a result, girls are allowed to live as boys for freedom and to protect and give status to the family when there is no boy in the family. The girl who lives as a boy will return to live as a girl when she reaches

Chapter 10 | Abuses Embedded in Cultural Traditions 190

puberty, but she may find she is not accepted as a girl when she returns. This bias for boys may hurt not only the girl living as a boy for that time but also her siblings because of the preferential treatment given to her when she lived as a 'boy.'

Think about what effects this may have on such societies and the children in particular who are victims. Give your thoughts

_____
_____
_____
_____

Witchcraft, Cults and Occults

It is believed by some people that some children and teenagers are used in witchcraft rituals or sacrificed in witchcraft practices. **Witchcraft** is the practice of magic, especially for evil purposes, using spells. It is also known as sorcery, black magic, the black arts, the occult, occultism, wizardry, witching, necromancy, voodoo, hoodoo, wonder-working, divination and Wicca.

Verifying and getting data on this is hard because this is a secret activity. Some children are also introduced to witchcraft practices, which can harm them. In some schools in Jamaica, for example, there were reports of children engaging in witchcraft activities by carrying 'guard rings' to protect them. People believe that wearing a guard ring gives them protective power. Beware, witchcraft activities are dangerous and will hurt you.

Chapter 10 | Abuses Embedded in Cultural Traditions **192**

The Daily Gleaner online, Published on Monday, April 4, 2022, and written by Paul H. Williams, Gleaner Writer, reported that a student was *"killed by a male schoolmate over claims that the deceased had stolen a friend's 'guard/power ring', and the claim by school administrators that the wearing or possession of such is prevalent among students, gripped the nation for a few days recently."*[13]

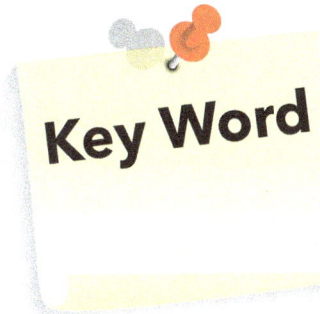

There have been reports of children whose parents are a part of cult groups, and the children are caught in these cultic practices. **There are two outstanding cases: 1. The Jim Jones Massacre-Georgetown, Guyana, and 2. The Waco Massacre, Waco, Texas.** In both cases, children were sexually abused or injured and have been traumatised because they and their parents were part of what is considered cultic practices.

The Waco siege, also known as the Waco massacre, was the siege by the U.S. federal government and Texas state law enforcement officials of a compound belonging to the religious cult known as the Branch Davidians between February 28 and April 19, 1993. Wikipedia[14]

Love Me Don't Hurt Me

Key Term

"**Jonestown massacre**" occurred on a remote settlement in Guyana established by the Peoples Temple, an American cult under the leadership of Jim Jones. On November 18, 1978, a total of 918 people died at the settlement. The majority drank a poisonous liquid as **"revolutionary suicide."** Seventy or more individuals at Jonestown were injected with poison, and a third of the victims were minors. Authorities concluded the deaths to be a mass murder-suicide or massacre.[15]

These types of belief systems and communities caused the death of the children whose families were a part of them.

You should research these two notorious historical cases and familiarise yourself with such groups' behaviour, as to be forewarned is to be forearmed.

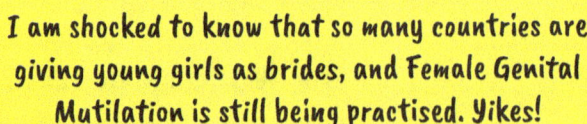

I am shocked to know that so many countries are giving young girls as brides, and Female Genital Mutilation is still being practised. Yikes!

I am sad that babies are being aborted or snatched from hospitals. Witchcraft and the Occult is real? OMG, we need to pray!

Chapter 10 | Abuses Embedded in Cultural Traditions

All the cultural practices mentioned above are harmful to teenagers.

LET'S TEST OUR LEARNING.

Below is a summary of the types of abusive situations that can cause you hurt or harm. They are considered to be evil by God. Be assured God hates them.

- When you do not have a good, active mother and father in a healthy relationship, it can also affect you badly.
- When you witness domestic abuse in the home, it can affect you negatively, and this can also hurt you.
- When parents and caregivers fail to protect you from abuse or all forms of harm and danger, this can cause you to be under-developed emotionally, socially or spiritually. It can also open you up to other forms of abuse because you grow up thinking that abuse is normal.
- When they expose you to danger, for example, if you are left unsupervised with members of the opposite sex or other 'unsafe'/abusive adults.
- When they fail to believe you when you are telling the truth about abuse
- Can you think of others?

_____
_____
_____
_____
_____
_____

Write in your own words what parents and guardians should provide for you as a part of their responsibilities towards you.

- _____
- _____
- _____
- _____

It is important to know that not all parents are negligent or hurt their children. Many loving parents do an excellent job rearing their children with care and protection. However, sometimes adults and other teenagers make you sad by hurting you.

If you believe that your parents, caregivers or guardians have failed you, causing hurt and pain, here are some of the things you can do:

Chapter 10 | Abuses Embedded in Cultural Traditions 196

- Forgive them, and ask God to help them change
- Seek help from a trusted adult
- Talk to your Guidance Counsellors
- Call a children's helpline for assistance
- Protect yourself as best as possible,
- Do not stay in an unsafe space.

You may not have been a victim of any of the above situations, but you can make a difference by raising awareness of such types of abuse and praying in groups for those teenagers in other countries who are.

Write a prayer below. Find a scripture to base your prayer on to remind God of His promise to protect those who need His protection.

_____
_____
_____
_____
_____
_____
_____
_____

11

Are You Aware of Your Environment?

LESSONS

1. Risk Assessment
2. Accidents in the Home
3. Accidents on the Road
4. Accidents at School
5. Natural Disasters
6. Epidemics, Pandemic & Infectious Diseases

Chapter 11 | Are You Aware of Your Environment? 198

Risk Assessment

"In simple terms, a risk is the possibility of something bad happening. Risk involves uncertainty about the effects/ implications of an activity with respect to something that humans value, often focusing on negative, undesirable consequences." Wikipedia.com

Accidents, Disasters, and Epidemics happen every day. However, if more care is taken by adults and teenagers alike, many of these can be prevented. A beneficial method is to assess the risk of the planned activity or situation

Key Term

beforehand and put the proper measures in place to make it safe.

A Risk Assessment is a systematic process of evaluating the potential risks involved in a projected activity or undertaking.[1]

When we approach our activities with an assessment of the potential risks involved, we stand a greater chance of avoiding the risk altogether or significantly reducing the harm or the extent of the impact on our lives or our surroundings. It may not come naturally to think like this, but once we have learned how to do it, it automatically becomes part of our thinking and being. Learning how to assess risk to protect ourselves as much as possible is very helpful.

Chapter 11 | Are You Aware of Your Environment?

To be proactive in making life safer, here are some key elements to include in your risk assessment.[1]

FIVE KEY ELEMENTS FOR A RISK ASSESSMENT		
1. Identify the Risk	Name the risk	Prevention(s)
2. Assess the Likelihood of the Risk		
3. Prioritise the Risk		
4. Evaluate the Impact of the Risk		
5. Review the Risk Regularly		Regularly review and update your risk assessment matrix as new risks emerge or existing ones evolve.

Accidents in the Home

In addition to the situations outlined in previous chapters, many other harmful/dangerous things happen to children, such as accidents at home, on the road, at school and in communities.

Have you ever had an accident at home? **Accidents at home** regularly happen and can range from minor to more severe, where children are badly injured or killed. Some accidents occur at home more during the summertime and during school breaks when children are out of school.

According to UNICEF, when it comes to Child and Adolescent Injuries, the following can happen to children:

- Unintentional injuries, such as road traffic crashes
- Drowning
- Falls
- Burns and scalds
- Poisonings.

These are the leading causes of death for children and adolescents worldwide. Globally, more than 1,600 children and adolescents below the age of 19 years die every day from preventable injuries. Of those injuries, road traffic crashes represent the leading cause of death.[2]

Some of these accidents happen at home when:

- You fall from stairs or climbing trees
- You choke on objects

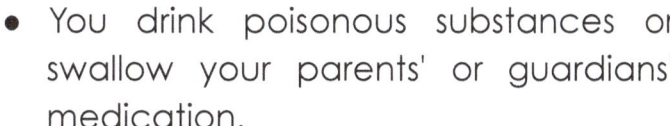

Key Terms

- You drink poisonous substances or swallow your parents' or guardians' medication.
- You are burnt and scalded by fire or hot liquids
- You are exposed to electrical hazards
- You are exposed to firearms that are not secured adequately at home.

Unsecured firearms can cause intentional or unintentional wounds or death to teenagers or others in the home.

The research data on accidental deaths caused by guns is alarming.

"4.6 million children in the United States live in homes with at least one gun that is loaded and unlocked."[3]

"Over the past decade, the firearm suicide rate among children and teens has increased by 66 per cent."[4]

> I usually tell my younger siblings to be careful. I'm constantly risk assessing their play area. I'd be traumatised if anything happened to them because of my carelessness.

Teenagers also have **drowning accidents** at different times of the year, especially during school breaks. They can drown in pools, ponds, lakes, water tanks, rivers, the sea, or any other body of water.[5]

Fires are also dangerous in homes, and there can be various reasons for fires. These can be due to electrical short-circuits, explosions or otherwise.

Teenagers can also start fires intentionally or unintentionally, thus setting the home ablaze. Home fires can kill them and others, even in adjoining homes. The unsafe use of cell phones, which can explode, curling irons, scented plug-in air fresheners and candles have also been known to cause injuries or deaths to teenagers.

As teenagers, you should always be supervised and not left alone. Some accidents can be avoided, so caregivers must ensure that everything is done to prevent these accidents and prevent children from being hurt. To prevent these accidents, adults need to be more aware and cautious of hazards and risks and take necessary steps to prevent injury.

I always try to be careful at home, school and in the community. I have younger siblings, so I always have to look out for them.

Chapter 11 | Are You Aware of Your Environment? **204**

Spot the hazards above.

State what should have been done in this case.

_____
_____
_____
_____
_____
_____
_____
_____
_____
_____

Accidents on The Road

A society that loves its teenagers should take great care to protect them and prevent harm as they use the road. For example, you must use the road daily whether you walk, ride, drive, take the bus or the train. Vehicular traffic has increased annually in almost every country.

Road accidents happen frequently and range from minor to severe injuries and deaths. Some of these cases are due to pedestrians or motorists not observing the road code, such as jaywalking, speeding, driving under the influence of drugs, not observing pedestrian crossings or other road signs, and driving faulty motor vehicles.

Key Term

Road safety is the responsibility of both adults and children. Adults must ensure that they are protected at all times. You are also responsible for observing the road code and signs to stay safe. Proper road signs must sometimes be erected for you and the other teenagers to observe.

Accidents at School

You spend your childhood years in school, and schools are responsible for ensuring your safety. Despite this, sometimes **accidents at school** occur, and some are very serious or fatal.

School accidents could be due to:
- Falls, slips, or trips
- Engaging in sporting activities or other commitments
- Lack of proper risk assessment in schools to eliminate danger
- Playing around that gets out of hand

Some of these accidents could have been prevented if people within the school community had been more careful. You can also be injured on school buses, which can be linked to school. School authorities are responsible for regular risk assessments of the school plant/grounds and facilities to remove or address all possible dangers and hazards.

Natural Disasters

Teenagers must be protected during natural disasters, environmental threats, *and hazards*.

You should be protected from things such as:

- Lead poisoning
- Carbon monoxide
- Pesticides and other toxic chemicals
- Polluted water
- Polluted air
- Other dangers

You should also be protected during the following natural disasters such as:

- Hurricanes
- Earthquakes
- Volcanic eruptions
- Mudslides and landslides
- Flooding
- Tsunamis
- Tornadoes
- Other _____

Natural disasters are potentially very harmful, so you must be protected during natural disasters. You may have to be removed from your home if it is damaged or destroyed.

In this case, you may be placed in public shelters; you should be protected from sex offenders and other harmful persons and given as much privacy as possible so that you are not exposed to predators or paedophiles who may be in the shelter with you.

Here is an exercise for you. Please write some other things that are harmful to you regarding environmental threats and natural disasters.

- _____
- _____
- _____
- _____
- _____

Infectious Diseases, Epidemics and Pandemics

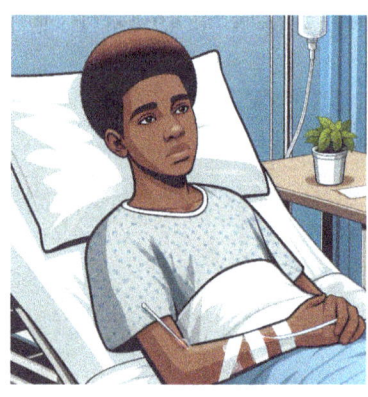

Epidemics, Pandemics and Infectious Diseases can all have devastating effects on children globally. "**Infectious diseases** are disorders caused by organisms — such as bacteria, viruses, fungi or parasites. Many organisms live in and on our bodies."[6] "**An epidemic** is a widespread occurrence of an infectious disease in a community at a particular time. For example "a flu epidemic" or "an epidemic of cholera."

"**A pandemic** is a widespread occurrence of an infectious disease over a whole country or the world at a particular time."[7] The COVID-19 pandemic was a prime example of all aspects of children's lives being affected: their health, education, home life, social and religious activities, etc. It is believed that more abuse of children took place during the COVID-19 pandemic period, especially when the children were under lockdown and spent months at home under various types of living conditions. Governments are responsible for protecting you against the effects of all these atrocities. Children are susceptible to all kinds of issues when these things happen.

What do the Scriptures say about accidents and diseases?

Psalm 36:7-8 says :
"7 God, your love is so precious! You protect people as a bird protects her young under her wings.
8 They eat the rich food in your house. You let them drink from your river of pleasure."

TEST YOURSELF

1. Use the risk assessment table in Lesson 1 to design your table around one risk chosen from each category we have studied.
    A. Accidents around the home
    B. Accident at school
    C.   Accident on the road
    D. Environmental threat or Natural disaster
    E. Epidemic/Pandemic/Infectious disease

Love Me Don't Hurt Me

GO TO the following website
https://staywise.co.uk/public/resource/hazard-house-game

Play Hazard Detective Online or

2. Design your Spot the Hazard Sheet. Include at least eight hazards around the home or at school.

Revision - Teenage Abuse

Chapter 11 | Are You Aware of Your Environment?

Across

4. Never returning for a child left behind
6. Selling a child as a commodity
8. Of a sexual nature regarding children
10. An adult who is sexually attracted to children
12. Causes you to feel bad about yourself
14. Allowed by law
15. Hiding or failing to deal with abuse
16. To do with the worship of God
17. Intended harm or injury
18. Regarding the anus
19. Taking a child across state borders
21. Texting sexually explicit messages

Down

1. Forced anal penetration
2. Another word for an adolescent
3. Forcing or manipulating others
5. Not wanting to have any contact with a child
7. Leaving a child unattended for inappropriate periods
9. Causing harm/injury to the body
11. To do with the internet
13. To do with how you feel
16. Forcing a child into sexual activity
20. Strategy to convince children to consent to sexual abuse

12

You Can Make a Difference!

LESSONS

1. Roles and Responsibilities
2. Encouragement and Motivation

Roles and Responsibilities

God spoke to the prophet Micah, as recorded in chapter 6, verse 8. He was outraged at the lack of responsibility that His people took for the wrongs that they did. He, however, gave a clear way back from all their bad habits and wrongdoings.

The prophet outlines below God's recommendations:

"8 The Lord has told you what is good. He has told you what he wants from you: Do

what is right to other people. Love being kind to others. And live humbly, trusting your God." **Micah 6:8**

This scripture tells us that regardless of what atrocities and evils are occurring around us as Christians, we are responsible for making a difference by doing what we know to be right to prevent and stop it. We must also live by a higher moral standard as an example to others. Regarding our discussion on abuse, here are things you can do to reduce abuse.

While you cannot avoid abuse totally, preventative actions can be taken, such as:

- Know the helpline to report abuses if there is one in your country
- Report abuse to parents, guardians or responsible adults. Sometimes, the adults close to you or looking after you hurt you. In such cases, call the national helpline.
- Do not take rides, food, or gifts from strangers.
- If you have doubts about a person's character, follow your instincts. Avoid them where possible, and talk to your parents or a responsible adult so that they can watch over you.

- Where possible, avoid lonely and dark shortcuts, and walk in groups when coming home from school if that is your mode of transportation.
- Be kind to other children; don't bully, body shame, or do any other harmful thing to them.
- If anyone tells you that what they are doing to you is a secret between you and them, you must report this to a responsible adult.
- Do not allow anyone to take a picture of your private parts.

Some Roles and Responsibilities of Parents, Guardians and Caregivers to reduce child abuse

Here are some affirmative actions that parents, guardians and caregivers can take to reduce child abuse.

- Parents, guardians and other caregivers must know what child abuse is and the dangers associated with it.
- Report cases of child abuse to the relevant authorities if you know or suspect that it is happening.
- Educate children by teaching them their rights in an age-appropriate way.
- Let them know that some body parts are private and should not be touched

by others, and they should not let anyone take pictures of them.
- Nurture, affirm, care for and build their self-esteem.
- Seek assistance from relevant organisations or agencies where necessary.
- Listen to them when they report the abusive behaviour of others.
- Encourage them in a non-judgmental way.
- Assure them that if they are abused, it is not their fault.

<u>The general rule is safety first. If in doubt check it out.</u>

Teenagers are precious to the Lord and must always be cared for.

What does the Bible say?

1. What do you think the scripture in **Psalm 8:2** says about God's view of children?

"You have taught children and babies to sing praises to you. This is because of your enemies. And so you silence your enemies and destroy those who try to get even."

_____
_____

2. Also, consider this scripture, **Psalm 127: 3.** What does it tell us about God's view of children?

"Lo, children are a heritage of the Lord, and the fruit of the womb is his reward."

_____
_____

Poem:# 1

Who is Minding the Children?

Who is minding the Children?

Are they not God's heritage?

Who is caring for them as selected arrows?

If not me or you, then who?

Someone has to do it; is it me or you?

Who is minding the Children?

As they go from day to day,

Some lost and suffering ones need our help.

Let's hear their cry and see their struggles

Rush quickly to meet their needs.

Who is minding the Children?

Some are lonely, abused, rejected and neglected.

Some are hungry, naked and abandoned.

These two poems show that adults should care for you.

Some are dysfunctional. Some are confused.

Hear their cry and reach out to them without delay.

Who is minding the Children?

Who is guiding them along life's way?

Who is rescuing them from paedophiles?

From traffickers and sexual exploiters?

Helpless, they are bound and gripped by fear and grief.

Who is minding the Children?

As they lay destitute by the wayside or in the home

In alleys and streets, motherless, fatherless, helpless!

Begging and crying for love and attention.

Their cries have touched the Father's heart.

Who is minding the Children?

Who may need a kind word or a loving touch?

A good deed done or to be pointed in the right way.

Allow them all to come to Jesus, who loves them.

Give them God's love, show them the Father's heart

Written by Jennifer Giscombe Williams
Published in the SHARE Magazine,[1]
September 2021©

1. Who is the writer speaking to in her poem?
2. Why does the writer repeat the poem's tile throughout the poem?
3. What is happening to children in the poem?
4. List some solutions to the problems identified in the poem.

Poem #2

Love Me

Love me, do not hurt me; this is what the Bible says

Love me, do not hurt me, not only today but every day

Love me, do not hurt me, as children we cry for help, not the belt

Love me, do not hurt me; to survive, I need your help

Love me, do not hurt me; provide the environment for me to thrive

Love me, do not hurt me so that I can remain alive

Love me, do not hurt me; this is part of my daily needs

Love me, do not hurt me; I am a righteous seed

Love me, do not hurt me; I am the arrow in the quiver

Love me, do not hurt me; this is a message for all caregivers

Love me, do not hurt me; I am underage

Love me, do not hurt me; I am the Lord's heritage

Love me, do not hurt me; do not let me cry or die

Love me, do not hurt me; forever, you must love me;

This is the Lord's desire.

Written by Jennifer Giscombe Williams
November 2023 ©

Let's test Our Learning.

1. Who is speaking in this poem?
2. What is the writer's objective in this poem?
3. The writer uses repetition again in this poem. How effective is that style in communicating?

The two poems above show that adults should be responsible for caring for you.

1. Choose two of the parents' roles and responsibilities mentioned in the poems above and write a script to role-play how you can carry out the advice given in the poems. During your role-play, you can choose to show either the negative or the positive side.

I was encouraged by this lesson. I love the poems. It helped me to reflect deeply on the topics discussed.

Chapter 12 | You Can Make a Difference! **222**

Encouragement and Motivation

God is The Good Father. He demonstrates how to parent throughout the Bible. We see that He deals with us in a balanced way. He motivates and encourages us when we please Him and tells us when we get it wrong. Like God does, it is important to be faithful to each other. When we make mistakes, God doesn't condemn us. He points out our shortcomings and shows us how to improve. Father God guides and counsels us as we strive towards improvement. He is our greatest cheerleader and motivator.

Paul, the Apostle, writes concerning how we should treat each other as children of God in **Ephesians 4:29-32**

"29 When you talk, do not say harmful things. But say what people need—words that will help others become stronger. Then, what you say will help those who listen to you. 30 And do not make the Holy Spirit sad. The Spirit is God's proof that you belong to him. God gave you the Spirit to show that God will make you

free when the time comes. 31 Do not be bitter or angry or mad. Never shout angrily or say things to hurt others. Never do anything evil. 32 Be kind and loving to each other. Forgive each other just as God forgave you in Christ."

Let's look at examples of how God motivates His children from scripture.

God Counsels Cain

'6 The Lord asked Cain, "Why are you angry? Why do you look so unhappy? 7 If you do good, I will accept you. But if you do not do good, sin is ready to attack you. Sin wants you. But you must rule over it."' **Genesis 4:6**

God Encourages Moses

'Then the Lord told Moses, "I will do what you ask. This is because I know you very well, and I am pleased with you."' **Exodus 33:12-13**

God Praises Isaiah

"Here is my servant, the one I support. He is the one I chose, and I am pleased with him. I will put my Spirit in him. And he will bring justice to all nations." **Isaiah 42:1**

God Praises and Glorifies Jesus

"Jesus heard the voice of God, the Greatest Glory. That was when Jesus received honour and glory from God the Father. The voice said, "This is my Son, and I love him. I am very pleased with him." **2 Peter 1:17**

Following God's good example, let us be encouragers and motivators.

Encouragement, motivation, and other interventions such as prayer, counselling, and spiritual deliverance can help a child build self-esteem, heal, and recover. Your dependence on the Lord can significantly assist you in healing and recovery from hurt.

You should get to know the Lord and build a solid relationship with Him. He is your Heavenly Father and should be your first choice if you have questions or are overwhelmed. As your Creator, He knows you best and always has your best interest at heart. What is incredible is that God always has time for you and is accessible through a simple prayer. He has no limitations in reaching you at your point of need. God is more than capable of helping you in every way necessary. He has given you earthly parents to care for you and help you grow up to be His pride and joy.

Here are some situations in which your parents should be prayerful, encouraging and caring towards you:

- When you are feeling down or depressed and can't get over it quickly
- When you are sick, and it is a lingering or long-term disease
- When you are/were abused
- At the death of a loved one, for example, a grandparent, sibling or friend
- When you lose a valuable item, whether it was lost or stolen
- When you fail at things that you do, for example, taking examinations
- When you did not do well in a sporting competition or activity
- For girls - at the start of the menstrual cycle, which can be frightening
- When going through puberty
- For boys - when you first experience a 'wet dream,' it can be embarrassing.

Tick the things below you would want your parents or caregivers to do to encourage you. Discuss with them the

need for them to encourage you in the following way:

- Help to build your confidence by speaking positive words over your life
- Show appreciation when you do positive things like assisting with younger siblings
- Participate in your activities such as attending graduations, sporting activities
- Allow you to engage in sporting activities rather than only in school work

Tick the phrases that you would love to hear from your parents and guardians when you believe that you have done well in some instances:

I noticed that you made your bed today; keep it up	Wow! That is great. Keep up the good work.	Good try; no one is perfect. Keep working at it.	I admire your efforts in working harder to complete your assignments on time
I am so proud of you today.	That is a brilliant idea to stay home and help with the baby today	You made my day when you did the laundry for your sister	That was a wise decision to apply to college

The Lord hears the prayers of a child. When Jesus was on earth, He encouraged His followers to be like little children who are usually humble. Let's read the following:

Matthew 18:1- 4

"1 *At that time, the followers came to Jesus and asked, "Who is greatest in the kingdom of heaven?"*
2 *Jesus called a little child to him. He stood the child before the followers.*
3 *Then he said, "I tell you the truth. You must change and become like little children. If you don't do this, you will never enter the kingdom of heaven.*
4 *The greatest person in the kingdom of heaven is the one who makes himself humble like this child."*

Here is a sample prayer that teenagers can pray:

A Teenager's Prayer

Dear Lord Jesus, thank You for loving and protecting me from harm and danger.

Thank You for watching over me day and night.

Thank You for giving Your angels the duty to watch over me and keep me safe daily.

Please help my parents and caregivers and others not to harm me.

Thank You for providing for my needs.

Please help me not to be afraid to report any form of abuse against me or other teenagers or children.

Please help me not to bully or hurt others.

Teach me how to treat people the way You want me to.

Show me how to love and accept others for who they are.

Give me the courage to accept and love myself and not allow myself to be mistreated.

Please keep the perverts away from me and other teenagers.

Please help me to obey my parents when they tell me to do the right thing.

Please keep me pure and help me to put my trust in You and not be ashamed of my faith in You.

Teach me to love You and to hate sin.

May Your will be done in my life and Your kingdom come. I pray in Jesus' name. Amen

For parents and guardians reading this book, here is a sample prayer you can pray.

Parents, Guardians and Caregivers Prayer

Dear Lord, thank You for placing my teenager in my care.

Help me to nurture them as You would want me to and not harm them or let others harm them.

Help me to be able to keep them from harm and danger and to protect them as You would.

Forgive me for not loving my teenager the way You love them and for causing their lives to be endangered.

Help me to do the right thing and report abuses against children and not hide the wrongdoings of others.

Give me wisdom, knowledge, and understanding to deal with them and address their needs appropriately.

Let Your will be done, and Your kingdom come into my life.

I pledge to love them as You would in Jesus' name.

Amen

Chapter 12 | You Can Make a Difference! **230**

I was encouraged by this chapter. I love the poems

Me too. I also love the prayers. It made this lesson personal for me.

"We have come to the end of our learning journey together we learnt a lot about abuse. Always remember safety first."

"Please join Abigail and myself as advocates against child abuse. Together we can make a difference."

Conclusion: Championing The Cause For Children's Justice

Conclusion 232

Dear teenagers, parents, guardians and caregivers, thank you for reading this book. I trust it has helped you understand how to interact with and nurture teenagers wholesomely. We have covered many actions that can hurt teenagers. While it was not an exhaustive discussion, it should give you a basic idea of most of the hurtful and traumatising situations that teenagers go through.

Like David and Abigail, our characters in the book have yet to experience everything that was discussed. David noted that as a male, he had similar experiences to Abigail, but some things were different for him because of his sex.

Abigail also noted that as a female, she

had similar experiences to David, but some things were different for her as a female. This shows us that some of the situations that teenagers face may not apply to others, but it will give them a basic understanding of some of the issues that teenagers face across the globe and how everyone can help protect them.

After reading this book, David and Abigail have decided to become Champions for Change in the fight to end child abuse. They have been using every opportunity to speak to their fellow students, their peers, teachers, parents, Guidance Counsellors, community members, and church members, among others, to create public awareness on the issue. Consider joining them in this worthy cause by doing what you can to spread awareness and challenge abuse where you see it.

Here are some suggestions-

The challenge remains for you to take the information you have learned and share it with your peers. Consider becoming champions of this Anti-Abuse Campaign to help eliminate child abuse.

You may also consider researching Child Abuse to keep abreast of the latest developments. You can make a massive difference by creatively presenting your findings to your school, church and community groups through songs, skits, plays, dub poetry, posters, short video clips, etc. You can also organise and host an annual Child Abuse Awareness Day event in your community.

If you found this book helpful, encourage other teenagers to purchase a copy to be informed. David and Abigail wish you all the best in your endeavours, pray that the Lord will protect you from danger, and ask that you exercise caution in your daily life and report child abuse to the relevant persons.

Remember to be self-aware and protect yourselves.

Trending terms

#lovemedonthurtme

As we end our study, here are some trending terms for you to use in your social media discussions. You must know and use these #hashtags well to protect yourself and others. Keep the movement to protect children going!

#STOPViolenceagaisntchildren

#Childprotection

#Notochildabuse

#Endchildslavery

#Nosexbeforemarriage

#Everychildmatters

#Childrights

#SelfHarmISanAlarm

#SelfloveNOTselfharm

#GodISLove

#Teenagersneedlovetoo

#Abstenancerocks!

#Jesusloveslittlechildren

#NoFGM

#YesJesusLovesMe

#SOSsombody

About the Author

Mrs. Jennifer Giscombe Williams is a Jamaican first-time author. She has been a Christian for almost 50 years. She has a Certificate in Business Studies from the Joint Examination of the London Chamber of Commerce and Industry and The Royal Society of Arts Examination Board. She also has a B.Sc in Management Studies, a M.Sc in Social Policy and a Diploma in Gender and Development Studies, all from the University of the West Indies.

Her other qualifications include a Certificate of Participation in Counselling - A Rights-Based Approach from the Coalition on the Rights of the Child, a Certificate of Attendance for the Workshop on the ' Inter-American system of human rights and the promotion and defence of the rights of the child', a Certificate of Completion on Holistic Child Development from Caribbean Graduate School of Theology and a Teacher's Certificate from Jamaica Child Evangelism Fellowship.

Mrs. Giscombe Williams has worked in the banking industry, gender and development field, and as a Human Resources Manager. During these years, she has gained extensive experience in addressing issues concerning gender-based violence, domestic violence, violence against women and girls, child abuse, and human resources issues, among other things.

She was also a Sunday School Teacher for some time. Her

most significant experience in working with child abuse came when she worked in the gender and development field, where she participated in matters relating to children in local, regional and international fora, including the United Nations. She has been engaged in discussions, planning and policies about childcare and child protection. She supervised the Research and Policy Department at the Bureau of Women's Affairs, Jamaica. She has also made several presentations on child abuse and gender-based violence at workshops in schools, communities and churches in her home country, Jamaica.

She was a Board member of the Women's Centre of Jamaica Foundation, which facilitates continuing education for girls who have dropped out of the formal school system due to pregnancy and return to the formal school system after the birth of their babies.

Mrs. Giscombe Williams has also sat on several Committees concerning matters relating to children. These include child labour and children in challenging circumstances.

She has now put some of her knowledge and experiences into this book. She firmly believes that children are to be loved and not harmed.

Answers

Chapter 5 - Crossword Puzzle

Across

2. FOSTERING
6. ABANDONED
7. MASKING
9. ADOLESCENCE
11. CONSENT
14. SMUGGLING
16. ANAL
17. GROOMING
18. SEXTING
20. PAEDOPHILES
21. RED
22. SHAMING

Down

1. CYBER
3. EMOTIONAL
4. TRAFFICKING
5. PRESSURE
8. NEGLECTED
10. CARNAL
12. INCEST
13. BULLYING
15. BUGGERED
16. ADOPTION
19. REJECTION

Chapter 6 - Crossword Puzzle

Across

5. TRADITIONAL
7. BARREL
9. ROLES
10. HOUSEHOLDS

Down

1. DONS
2. FAMILY
3. SIBLINGS
4. MIGRATION
6. VALUES
8. BARREL

Chapter 11 - Crossword Puzzle

Across

4. ABANDONMENT

6. TRAFFICKING

8. CARNAL

10. PAEDOPHILE

12. SHAMING

14. CONSENT

15 MASKING

16. SPIRITUAL

17. ABUSE

18. ANAL

19. SMUGGLING

21. SEXTING

Down

1. BUGGERY

2. TEENAGERS

3. BULLYING

5. REJECTION

7. NEGLECT

9. PHYSICAL

11. CYBER

13 EMOTIONAL

16. SEXUAL

20. GROOMING

Endnotes

Chapter 2

[1] Martín-Rodríguez, A., Tornero-Aguilera, J., López-Pérez, P., Clemente-Suárez V., & Clemente-Suárez, V. (2022). The Effect of Loneliness in Psychological and Behavioral Profile among High School Students in Spain. Sustainability, 14(1), 168.

[2] https://www.merriam-webster.com/dictionary/Generation%20Z

[3] Maragkopoulou, K. (2021). DIGITAL MEDIA AND ENGLISH LANGUAGE DEVELOPMENT OF DUAL LANGUAGE LEARNERS IN KINDERGARTEN. https://doi.org/10.23860/thesis-maragkopoulou-kassandra-2021

[4] Malik, M. S. (2018). Male body image across the life course: A mixed methods study. https://core.ac.uk/download/161893952.pdf

[5] Veris Top Surgery. https://www.timeofx.com/veris-top-surgery

Chapter 3

[1] https://www.psychologytoday.com/us/blog/lifetime-connections/201505/13-red-flags-potentially-toxic-friendship

[2] https://www.audleyvillages.co.uk/25-tips-for-social-fitness?utm_source=google&utm_medium=cpc&utm_campaign=pmax_scarcroft&utm_keyword=&utm_content=gen-property&gclid=CjwKCAjwh4-wBhB3EiwAeJsppD92irOEJl2-cogbh8oSX5BydmJ8eFiolyHJ51JSL-RQJJWgGL8bexoClt4QAvD_BwE

Chapter 4

[1] UNICEF- October 2002 https://www.ohchr.org/en/instruments-mechanisms/Instruments/convention-rights-child

[2] A Jamaica Coalition on the Rights of the Child Publication. Taken from a teacher's workbook entitled Awareness Building on Child Rights Based on the Convention on the Rights of the Child by Lloyd Stanley and Carol V. Samuels:

[3] https://www.unicef.org/protection

Chapter 5

[1] https://www.who.int/teams/social-determinants-of-health/violence-prevention/global-status-report-on-violence-against-Children-2020

[2] https://www.cdc.gov/violenceprevention/youthviolence/bullyingresearch/fastfact.html#:~:text=Bullying%20is%20a%20frequent%20discipline,and%20primary%20schools%20(9%25

[3] https://languages.oup.com/google-dictionary-en

[4] https://legaldictionary.net/date-rape/

[5] https://stmlearning.com/news/all-blog-posts/evidence-collection-in-sexual-assault-cases/#:~:text=Oral%2C%20anal%2C%20vaginal%2C%20and,be%20collected%20from%20the%20victim

[6] https://data.unicef.org/topic/child-health/adolescent-health/

[7] https://www.iom.int/sites/g/files/tmzbdl486/files/documents/counter-migrant-smuggling.pdf

[8] The Subtle Power Spiritual Abuse written by David Johnson and Jeff VanVonderen.

Chapter 6

[1] https://www.jamaicaobserver.com/editorial/a-different-approach-please-for-the-childrens-sake/

[2] https://www.thechillmom.com/2020/10/working-moms-raise-more-independent-kids

Chapter 7

[1] Substance Use Treatment / Counseling Archives - SoulBeing. https://soulbeing.com/therapy/substance-use-treatment-counseling/

[2] https://www.therecoveryvillage.com/teen-addiction/drug/commonly-abused-drugs/

[3] https://www.theguardian.com/society/2019/nov/14/witchcraft-and-black-magic-contribute-to-increase-in-child-abuse

[4] https://www.mayoclinic.org/healthy-lifestyle/tween-and-teen-health/in-depth/teens-and-social-media-use/art-20474437#:~:text=Lead%20some%20teens%20to%20form,such%20as%20anxiety%20and%20depression.

[5] cnbc.com/josephine-bila

[6] https://www.aacap.org/AACAP/Families_and_Youth/Facts_for_Families/FFF-Guide/Teen-Suicide-010.aspx

Chapter 8

[1] https://www.unicef.org/protection/programmes

Chapter 9

[1] https://learningenglish.voanews.com/a/in-mexico-Teenagers-as-young-as-10-recruited-by-drug-cartels/6275555.html

[2] https://jamaica-gleaner.com/article/news/20221101/children-implicated-875-major-crimes-over-four-year-period

[3] https://jamaica-gleaner.com/article/lead-stories/20220206/caught-middle

[4] https://en.wikipedia.org/wiki/Chibok_schoolgirls_kidnapping#:~:text=On%20the%20night%20of%2014, Chibok%20in%20Borno%20State%2C%20Nigeria

[5] https://www.cbsnews.com/news/nigeria-mass-abduction-boko-haram-girls-kidnapped-reports-isis/

[6] https://www.unicef.org/protection/children-recruited-by-armed-forces

[7] https://www.unicef.org.uk/wp-content/uploads/2016/02/UnicefChildSoldiersbriefing_UKweb.pdf

[8] https://www.unicef.org/protection/violence-against-children-in-school

Chapter 10

[1] https://www.unicef.org/protection

[2] https://www.unicef.org/protection/child-marriage

[3] Child Marriage FAQs - World Vision UK

https://www.worldvision.org.uk › our-work › child-marr...

[4] https://www.worldvision.org/child-protection-news-stories/10-worst-places-child-marriage

[5] https://www.unfpa.org/female-genital-mutilation#:~:text=UNFPA%20estimates%2068%20million%20girls, practice%20due%20to%20COVID%2D19.Unfpa.org

[6] https://www.ncbi.nlm.nih.gov/pmc/articles/PMC10372806/
Korean J Fam Med. 2023 Jul; 44(4): 183–188.
Published online 2023 May 16. doi: 10.4082/kjfm.22.0206
PMCID: PMC10372806
PMID: 37189262
Period Poverty: A Neglected Public Health Issue

[7] https://www.ncbi.nlm.nih.gov/pmc/articles/PMC10372806/#:~:text=Period%20poverty%20can%20be%20defined,

menstrual%20hygiene%20education%20%5B6%5D.

[8] https://en.wikipedia.org/wiki/Child_abduction

[9] https://jamaica-gleaner.com/article/lead-stories/20150301/pimp-parents-persist-many-st-thomas-children-forced-prostitution

[10] https://www.voanews.com/a/east-asia-pacific_philippines-parents-pimp-out-their-children-covid-job-losses-mount/6199166.html

[11] https://jlrjs.com/child-prostitution-in-india/

[12] https://www.encyclopedia.com/social-sciences/encyclopedias-almanacs-transcripts-and-maps/gender-preferences-children#:~:text=Son%20preference%20is%20particularly%20strong,%2C%20South%20Korea%2C%20and%20China.

[13] https://jamaica-gleaner.com/article/news/20220404/tread-carefully-guard-rings

[14] https://en.wikipedia.org/wiki/David_Koresh

[15] https://www.rollingstone.com/feature/jonestown-13-things-you-should-know-about-cult-massacre-121974

Chapter 11

[1] https://languages.oup.com/google-dictionary-en/

[2] https://www.unicef.org/health/injuries#:~:text=On%20average%2C%20more%20than%20600,rates%20in%20sub%2DSaharan%20Africa.

[3] https://everytownresearch.org/issue/child-and-teens/

[4] https://everytownresearch.org/stat/the-firearm-suicide-rate-among-children-and-teens-has-increased-by-59-percent/

[5] https://www.freepik.com/free-vector/life-guard-flat-banners-set_3907725.htm#fromView=search&page=2&position=2&uuid=09f71389-ccc0-40c5-8b19-6b1770b28f12

[6] https://www.mayoclinic.org/diseases-conditions/infectious-diseases/symptoms-causes/syc-20351173

[7] google dictionary
[1] https://www.ask.com/news/key-elements-include-risk-assessment-matrix-template?utm_content=params%3Aad%3DdirN%26qo%3DserpIndex%26o%3D740004%26ag%3Dfw&ueid=FC20659A-6FBF-4D8D-BEB2-B6244E3235CE

[1] https://issuu.com/thesharemagazine/docs/share_magazine_vol9-iss4/41

www.ingramcontent.com/pod-product-compliance
Lightning Source LLC
Chambersburg PA
CBHW082200070526
44585CB00020B/2217